Wanderlust in Suburbia

and Other Reflections on Motherhood

New York Times & USA Today Bestselling Author
MARILYN BRANT

Twelfth Night Publishing

Copyright © 2015 Marilyn B. Weigel

All rights reserved.

Cover Design: Sterling Design Studios

ISBN-13: 978-0-9893-1609-5

DEDICATION

For Mothers - one & all & everywhere - especially mine.
Thanks, Mom.

CONTENTS

About This Book	i
Homespun Hearts (poem)	1
My Little Everything	2
An Ordinary Day	5
Leaning Toward Optimism	8
The Courage of Courtesy	12
Appearances of Motherhood (poem)	16
A Tribute to Fathers	17
Mommy Out of Context	21
Raising a "Very Active" Boy	26
In Appreciation of Grandparents	30
Fingerprints on the Windowpane (poem)	34
The Power of Gratitude	36
Thankfulness and Expectations	41
Blessings and Insanity During the Holidays	45
The Best Holiday Gifts Ever	50
Sneaking Up on the Holidays	54
One Rotation (poem)	59

Resolving to Do Something "Big"	60
On Being Extraordinary in an Ordinary Life	64
Spring Cleaning	69
Our Own Drummers	73
Insomnia (poem)	77
On Mothers, Daughters, Sons, and Worrying	78
Remembering Unstructured Time	83
Wanderlust in Suburbia	88
Journals as Time Machines of Motherhood	93
Excerpt from THE ROAD AND BEYOND	97
Other Books by Marilyn Brant	123
About the Author	126

ABOUT THIS BOOK

Dear Reader,

Maybe it's just my personal experience talking, but I don't think many women—even those of us who've spent a fair bit of time with other people's children—realize the degree to which our lives will change when we become mothers ourselves. We might *predict* a major transitional period or *imagine* the big lifestyle adjustments ahead, but there's so much we simply cannot *know* in advance, despite our enthusiastic (or, in my case: zealous, bordering on fanatical) attempts to prepare for this incredible new role.

No matter how organized I tried to be after my son's birth, there were surprises waiting around every corner. More often than not, any carefully constructed plans I had would need to be revised or tossed out altogether. And each new season with my baby brought a slew of revelations and discoveries that I'd wrestle with and, finally, manage to assimilate, only to have to relearn everything a few months later when he grew into a new stage. True for many moms, I'm sure.

Naturally, being a writer by both profession and inclination, I filled up journal after journal and wrote dozens of poems and magazine pieces in an attempt to wrap my mind around all that had become "motherhood" to me...in its beautiful, changeable, strange, and indefinable glory.

Prior to my decision to stay at home with our newborn son, I'd been a full-time elementary school teacher in the northern Chicago suburbs. I'd earned an M.A. in educational psychology, researching the connection between "Creativity" and "Culture," and I *loved* this topic. I took pride in introducing my students to activities that would stretch them creatively. I adored working with so many talented children every year. And I tried to come up with new ways to make learning more exciting and challenging for everyone in the classroom.

So, when I began my freelance writing career, which started when my son was a few months old and spanned nearly a decade, I focused on writing for parenting magazines—penning articles packed with enrichment ideas. The features I wrote were geared toward moms and dads who wanted to do fun extension projects at home with their young children, often using the arts to bring an added dimension to core subject areas. I'd even begun work on a nonfiction "activity book" for parents and teachers. Given my love of this area, I was convinced this was my calling.

But—in what I quickly realized would be a frequent occurrence as a new mom—something unexpected happened.

Much as I enjoyed putting together these educational articles, I found myself increasingly drawn to writing essays on the subject of motherhood instead. Every day I spent at home with my infant (then toddler, then preschooler—oh, how fast he grew!) seemed to provide even more parental adventures and observations. I had a wealth of writing material at hand just by opening my eyes and stepping out of bed each morning, and I never stopped craving a way to process these experiences. I talked endlessly to my fellow mom friends at the park. I devoured memoirs written by other mothers. And I loved getting to share my personal impressions with an understanding readership when my own essays were accepted for publication.

Motherhood had inducted me into a clan of women who

had stories to tell…about themselves, their children, their families, their career ambitions, their day-to-day experiences and, most of all, the way they merged their daydreams, their passions, and their creative lives with their role as someone's "Mommy." It also led me down a completely different writing path, one toward contemporary women's fiction and my first publishing contract. Motherhood was, in fact, the reason I became a novelist. Somewhere along the journey, during those early years at home with my son, I realized that I, too, had a few stories to tell.

Most of the regional and national parenting magazines I wrote for back at the dawning of the 21st Century are, sadly, no longer in print, and these previously published essays plus the few poems that I've assembled here (all organized loosely around the seasons) are not available in any other format now—paper or electronic. So, the time was right to finally make this compilation of my favorites.

It's being released this year in honor of Mother's Day, and it's my little tribute to our mothers and our grandmothers. To our women friends. And to all of us as well. It's my dearest hope that these reflections will bring a smile of recognition to your lips and add a bit of joy to your heart as you read them…and, perhaps, think about those moms you love.

Best wishes & thanks for picking up this collection~
Marilyn Brant
Chicago, May 2015

HOMESPUN HEARTS

Dancing children twirl
around the room of my heart.
Blur us together.

MY LITTLE EVERYTHING

When Andy Gibb sang "I Just Want To Be Your Everything," chances are that we—those of us with our ear to the radio in the late 1970s—didn't attribute much philosophic insight to his claim. But X, Y, and Z generations later, I find myself looking back with fondness onto the simplicity of that very human desire. Andy, of course, was singing about male-female relationships, but—having left the days of disco behind long ago and, more recently, entered the days of diapers—I have a newfound perspective drawn from those words: For a while, most parents want to be their child's everything.

Actually, "want" is a deceptive term. "Must" is a more accurate descriptor, at least initially. This is especially true for mothers.

While pregnancy is a time of immense physiological changes, who could ignore the psychological and emotional transformations we must also make? We invite our unborn children to overtake our bodies as they grow inside of us. We nourish them with every fiber of our being. We labor to give birth to them and, in the process, release a part of our heart—as well as our flesh—out into a potentially harsh world, unsure of what will be encountered. We know this world is not always safe, nor is it always fair. We know they will be dependent upon us for years and not only for the basics of food, clothing, and shelter, but also for love, hope, inspiration, compassion, nurturing, protection, and guidance. We want to give them everything. Every part of ourselves that we can give to ease their way.

There's a catch, of course.

To truly give them what they need, we must progressively loosen our grip and, eventually, let go. This is something I struggled with throughout my pregnancy and my child's infancy. Perhaps for some parents the challenge of release is greater than for others. After all, each of us brings to parenthood our unique strengths and also the lessons we must, in the end, learn ourselves. I have friends who, after a hug and an affectionate kiss goodbye, can set their children free…still praying every moment for their babies' safety and happiness, but not clinging in a manner that might hinder their growth. I, on the other hand, hear the phrase, "We teach our children to walk and they walk away," and I burst into tears at the inevitability.

I'm learning.

I know as an adult that no one person can meet all of my needs. Even among my loved ones and dearest friends, I know there are times when I need the special gifts and priceless qualities of one individual more than the others. Why should my son be any different in his needs and wants?

I don't pretend to always enjoy my transition to the periphery, though, even as I applaud his steps toward independence. As he continues to grow, change, and develop into a young person with opinions in his own right, his circle will widen. Slowly he will no longer remember that once, for a blissful and simultaneously overwhelming period of time, I was his everything.

But I will remember.

And, lovingly, I will hold onto that memory as I watch him enter into the world to gather his own friends, revel in his own strengths, master his own lessons, and sing his own songs. As parents that is our privilege and, to me, it means everything.

AN ORDINARY DAY

Prior to the birth of my son and our consequent decision for me to become an at-home mom, my life afforded its share of adventures. Since my husband and I were both teachers, we traveled together during the summer vacations, dined at our favorite restaurants, and saw plays and musical performances. We also experienced the daily school-year excitement of humorous student anecdotes, complicated staff relationships, and the frequently occurring technology-gone-bad situations. Everyone could readily understand these events—there was a certain natural recognition, a standard chronology to those stories, nothing wildly abstract or requiring much in the way of imagined projection. Ultimately, life was never too dramatic, but we had just enough excitement to still be considered fairly interesting.

My husband, when asked, can still recount work stories as a means of relating to others in conversation—although the days of travel, dining and plays are long gone. I, however, do not have that conversational luxury. This is especially apparent when someone telephones.

"Hi. How are you all? What have you been doing today?"

"*We're fine, thanks. It's been an ordinary day: cooking, dishes, bills—and a lot of playtime with the baby.*"

"Is he doing anything other than crawling yet?"

"*Well, he's chewing on the phone cord right now.*"

"Ah-ha, I mean anything else, anything *big*?"

"*No.*"

"Oh."

And so it goes. I had tried to explain the other stuff—the intangibles—but they rarely came across quite right. As I heard myself speak about my day to family and friends, even *I* started to believe that my life was as shockingly boring as it appeared.

The routine was extremely predictable. There was nothing *big* that I could think to write much about, even in my nightly journal. Any true changes were marked by degrees of subtlety since our little boy's major milestones (i.e., rolling, sitting, crawling, etc.) rarely happened "overnight." Fortunately, there were no great traumas or Herculean problems—just a normal, average, uneventful day—virtually every day. It was blissfully peaceful but undoubtedly ordinary and uninteresting to the rest of the world.

In the midst of yet another typical day, I remembered a poster that used to hang proudly in my third-grade classroom: "Learn to Discover What Turns the Ordinary in the Extraordinary!" It carried with it all the clarity of vision and optimism so characteristic of a child's world. I had loved it as a teacher and, yet, had momentarily overlooked it as a mother.

What could be more eventful, unusual or extraordinary than watching my baby attempt to figure out the mysteries of his world? What adult would think of an empty milk carton as an object of great wonder and not just something for the recycling bin? Who else looks at reflected sunlight on the floor and reaches out to grab it, amazed by its ability to resist capture each time? Then there are unbelievably strange sounds: lawn mowers, dishwashers, vacuum cleaners, chirping birds, Grandma's voice...how different they all are! There's the unparalleled thrill of movement—in cars or strollers, or especially by the power of one's own little legs, jumping up and down with sheer delight.

Every day, our child sees, hears and senses each and every thing he encounters so freshly. He approaches life with such curiosity and finds joy, excitement and surprise in the most ordinary of objects or events. Most amazingly, this wise little master teaches me to rediscover the wonder in everything around me that I took for granted and, perhaps, never really saw before when I was so caught up in more interesting-sounding and seemingly eventful moments. Every day is another extraordinary day as seen through the eyes of my little miracle. But to explain this incredible day to others on the telephone?

No. C'mon over instead. You just have to be here.

LEANING TOWARD OPTIMISM

Once, in our newly married, pre-parental days, my husband and I were vacationing in Northern France. We liked to consider ourselves deep, serious people throughout much of the year, having spent—as teachers—many months juggling pressing student concerns with demanding academic requirements. But this was summer. It was a time for rest, relaxation, and a wild jump into fun foreign culture. We took this initiative to heart. A reward to ourselves for a school year successfully concluded.

Thus, while we were diligent in visiting virtually every historical site in Normandy—from the infamous WWII beaches to the Bayeux Tapestry—our days were interspersed with crepe or cider taste testing, long walks around castle ruins, and window-shopping at patisseries. We were happy.

Back at our quaint, postcard-perfect inn after one such joyful day, I was flipping through a Parisian women's magazine I'd come across in the lobby. Bypassing fashion articles and other perceived drivel, I settled down with a story on the performing arts. Now, my French, while never extraordinarily fluent, was adequate enough for me to be insulted by a line I read about midway through the piece. It was about Americans. The young female writer was making the point that American audiences didn't appreciate certain theater productions because "happy endings are so important to them."

Upon translating this, I stopped mid-column and reread that line several times before finally calling out to my husband, "Hey, listen to this!"

We bristled at the snub—certainly intentional, we felt. We believed, much like Meg Ryan's character in *When Harry Met Sally*, that we could be as dark and brooding as anyone out there. Of course we were generally optimistic. We wanted the good guys to win, the ugly duckling to turn into a beautiful swan, and the poor servant girl to finally get to be the belle of the ball, but was that a reason to assume we couldn't handle the alternative?

Finally, recovering our good humor with the help of some hard cider and a chocolate pastry, we dismissed the remark, attributing it to an unfair stereotype of Americans held by "a snobby contingency of Old World elitists who'd convinced themselves that those of us living across the pond lacked culture."

Au contraire! I thought, still indignant.

Now, some years later, while I can't speak to the current beliefs of elitists (Old World or otherwise), nor would I deign to put words in the mouths of my fellow American citizens, I feel I've grown to accept my inclination to such hopefulness, beyond merely a superficial preference for a "happy" versus "sad" ending.

I'll admit, I smile to myself when I think back to that article...to that time period. Perhaps the writer had been aware of an element of our nation's personality that I'd chosen to overlook: We Americans *do* appear, quite often, to be pretty happy-go-lucky in the eyes of the rest of the world. Hollywood turns out a slew of movies every year with the latest big-name stars featured in films with upbeat endings. And we continually admire the underdog athletes who help their teammates come from behind to take the championship or the Olympic gold. But every country treasures their heroes, their triumphs, their Cinderella Stories.

Or, maybe there was a human element that both the writer and I were trying to be too hip to value. Perhaps that adolescent desire for cool detachment was still too much with us then. After all, it's hard to be taken seriously in any art—especially writing or drama—if your work appears simplistically cheerful or lacks a sharpened sense of cynicism. But, whatever the reason for her argument or mine, discussion of that kind somehow smacks of either innocence or ignorance now. Parenthood has changed it all for me.

Currently, as a mother and, I hope, as a more aware citizen, I don't even want to *pretend* to be dark and brooding. I openly and unabashedly want happy endings in as many situations as they can be arranged. I want Planet Earth to be well cared for and pollution-free, with clean air and water, restored rainforests, and an abundant animal population. I want the needs of the world's children—my son's peers—to be so well fulfilled that they all grow up to be healthy and loving adults. I want to see our amazing human creative potential directed in positive channels. I want to short-circuit apathy, elitism in any form, and behavior that pulls people apart instead of bonds them together. And, yes, I even want everyone to sing, sing a song...

Happiness may not provide much intrigue or dramatic flair, but I would joyously forgo any sense of theatrical discontent to bring back to all of us that blissful illusion in childhood when belief in happy endings is unquestioned—the natural and expected outcome.

As for all of the famous historical sites I saw abroad, I cannot think of them now as independent entities or as separate from our current history; I no longer have the luxury of such detachment in that arena either. They are linked in time's memory to us and to each other. The earth and its history have all become part of an interconnected cultural dance in my mind—the way it always had been in reality, I guess, whether or not I was willing to see it.

Yet another lesson parenthood has taught me: We are not alone in life's struggles. Ah, but we can all hope for the best, can't we?

And, somehow, I suspect that the French writer—especially if she is now a mother, too—feels the same way.

THE COURAGE OF COURTESY

Some years back, when I was working as an elementary classroom teacher, I asked for volunteers to help with an original play the class was performing. A throng of parents descended to assist with the production—from constructing costumes to sending in props to organizing a feast for the post-show "cast party." A couple of parents were memorable in the most remarkable of ways. They seemed to anticipate my needs before I could articulate them, and all of us in the classroom benefited as a result of their thoughtfulness.

By contrast, there was another parent that I also remember distinctly. "I want to help!" she pleaded, noting the quickly filled sign-up sheets. "What can I do? What can I bring?"

I suggested a simple task: Sending in two props I needed for rehearsal the following week that she, because of her job, could acquire more easily than most parents. She drew her eyebrows together and said, "That's not much... What? Don't you trust me?" Her lips twisted into a smile to alert me of her jest.

I assured her that this was all I needed for the time being, but it was significant. Then I thanked her for her participation and told her how much I was looking forward to her assistance.

The next week came and went, and the items I'd requested of her were nowhere to be found. Not wanting to put her child on the spot by asking more than twice if the youngster's mother had sent in any supplies, I called the woman directly.

"Oh, I forgot," she said pleasantly. "Sorry. Can I send them in tomorrow?"

I told her that it would be very helpful and reiterated how valuable her contribution was to us.

The next day nothing. The day after that also nothing. The performance date was a mere three weeks away, and the students had yet to rehearse with the props this parent had pledged to bring in.

I left the mother a polite phone message saying that I appreciated her desire to help, but she no longer had to worry about the props in questions. I could modify accordingly.

She called me back the following afternoon, breezily insisting I could count on her. "Tomorrow for sure," she said.

The next day nothing.

I asked myself a series of questions: Was this not a worthy enough task for her? Was she just stunningly forgetful, despite the fact that this show was all her child and every student in class could talk about for most of the spring? Was she playing a passive-aggressive game to get back at me for some unknown educational infraction? Was she simply overloaded with other activities, having taken on too much and prioritized too little? Was I someone she considered expendable?

I never got a clear answer, but I got the props—a few days later—from a different, more reliable source.

Still, dealing with this type of behavior is hard for me when I encounter it, and I encounter it altogether too often. The friend who says she'll call you next Sunday then fails to do so. The classmate who vows on his life he'll help you with a project then leaves you in a last-minute lurch. The employer who claims she'll write you a letter of recommendation then manages to forget to send it. The mechanic who says he'll meet you at an agreed upon location then doesn't show up...or phone in an apology...or explain extenuating circumstances. It's small insensitivities such as these that chip away at our confidence in humanity.

On occasion, a part of me almost hopes to be able to attribute this type of behavior to a flashier target than mere discourtesy: Sexism, ageism, game playing, prejudices based on religious, racial, or ethnic differences. But I don't honestly believe those were the actual excuses—at least not for the majority of people I've counted on to fulfill promises. I didn't consider that parent a "bad person" then, nor do I now, despite my continued belief that her actions were irresponsible and inconsiderate. Even today, I'm hopeful that was a one-time violation. That she's redeemed herself in further interactions with others and been true to her word or, at least, declined to continue in a charade of compliance.

Reflecting, I can offer only one conclusion: To honor each other, we must have the courage to be genuinely courteous. To say "yes, absolutely" with certainty or "sorry, no" with equal conviction. People so often lament that "big" changes must be made to bring greater peace and harmony to our planet. We feel overwhelmed and don't know where to start. Yet, if these are our values, why not begin in the nearest of locations? Treat those around you as valuable—whether or not helping them makes you look good, furthers your career/pocketbook/social agenda, or relegates your actions to the realm of anonymity. If you are in the position to help someone, and want to help, do so. If you can't or don't, be brave enough to decline gracefully. It's said that the measure of a society is the way its strong members treat those who are weak or powerless—the elderly, young, sick, subordinate, underprivileged. And who is in the "strong" position, and who is not, is subject to change.

To successfully lead a family, school, or nation requires a collective societal value—built individual by individual—in which each member is honorable enough to be genuinely courteous, even when it's difficult.

It's a rare, but needed, courage.

APPEARANCES OF MOTHERHOOD

So, this is Motherhood:
Hair unkempt, unnoticed
Clothes baggy, wrinkled, stained
Complexion unscrubbed, ignored, radiant with adoration
Eyes drooping, exhausted, amazed, shining
Body flabby from maternal changes, fertile ground
overwhelmed by an abundant harvest
Arms aching, sore, cradle of love and comfort
Heart overflowing with joy, contentment, peace
Soul certain, steadfast, soaring.

A TRIBUTE TO FATHERS

For several years now I've been aware of fatherhood getting a bad rap. While in some cases this may be deserved, there are so many circumstances (fortunately) where it is not. Yes, the numbers of absentee dads are on the rise; that's true. And we've all heard of the problems caused by child-support dodgers. But, lost in all the bad press is this: There are some amazing, wonderful, caring fathers out there—near, far, and everywhere—who also deserve to be recognized for their unfailing devotion and commitment.

I personally know more than a few such heroes and am ever grateful to them:

They are the fathers who offer to take the children to the playground, or out for breakfast, so "Mommy" can sleep late sometimes.

They are the fathers who are truly there in sickness and in health—cradling a congested infant at 3 a.m. on an early Tuesday or dashing to the pharmacy to pick up children's Tylenol at a moment's notice.

They are the fathers who cancel or postpone their personal plans in order to take an excited youngster to a birthday party. They are dads who consistently put their son's or daughter's needs ahead of their own and don't expect the world to slather them in praise for it.

They are the fathers who have learned to change a baby's diaper—perhaps not one-handed but at least without complaint. They warm bottles of formula or breast milk, hunt for misplaced "binkies" with the intensity of a hound, learn to sing lullabies as well as the entire *Dragon Tales* soundtrack, and struggle to dress a squirmy, increasingly independent toddler.

They are the fathers who—regardless of life's misfortunes, personal difficulties, or situations of divorce—are still there to celebrate their children's special occasions with fanfare. And they're also there to listen and counsel on days of no particular importance, no calendar-marking holiday, but simply because a child might need them.

They are the fathers who punctuate their child's life with little surprises—a movie together, an unexpected ticket to a baseball game or theatrical performance, a long-desired toy that encouraged a burgeoning interest, a story of the past told with enthusiasm, or a project shared that would have been easier done alone.

They are the fathers who strive, with a saint's patience, to teach a child a new skill: From tying shoelaces to tying slipknots, from word definitions to word processing, from driving a car to driving a golf ball down the course. By helping their children with chess, art, gardening, building, sports, music, or more, these dads experience their hobbies with fresh eyes, newfound perspective, and a delight in sharing a part of themselves in an incomparable manner.

They are the fathers who read to their children, enriching their youngsters' minds and imaginations in the process. They have rousing discussions together, demonstrating critical thinking, humor, and creativity, as well as the social nuances of conversation.

They are the fathers who recognize sadness or worry in the voice of their young college student and call back long distance just to see if he or she is "okay." They read between the lines in letters sent home and write notes of encouragement in return. They learn how to modify their behavior and advice—as their little baby becomes a child, then a teen and, finally, an adult.

They are the fathers who, even when decidedly non-chef-like by nature, rally every culinary skill they possess to prepare a healthy meal for their children. Or, if more talented with spatulas, steam cookers, or skewers, they work to make dinner a gourmet feast.

They are the fathers who listen to school stories and knock-knock jokes again and again and again...without visible exasperation (or maybe only a little). When they reach their breaking point, they try to mask their frustration...or attempt to tactfully change the subject.

They are the fathers who are also grandfathers or godfathers. They, in an act of kindness and generosity, offer to step in sometimes to give their adult children or close friends a much-needed reprieve from *their* own youngsters.

They are the fathers who are good sportsmen, wonder-filled world-of-make-believe pretenders, astounding strategy game players, exuberant chasers, vibrant storytellers, great ride givers, and the very best models of masculinity for both their sons and their daughters. Their children hope to either be like them—or know others like them—someday.

They are the fathers who teach their child to be respectful of differences in others, to be compassionate toward all, and to dream big dreams.

They are the fathers who know how to praise their child for accomplishments made, but also know that worldly achievements are superficial and frequently temporary; thus, they also reward their child for simply being a caring, generous, thoughtful individual—the person they helped to raise.

They are the fathers who willingly share their values, their time, their love, their passions, and their insights with their child whenever asked, and especially when not asked, but needed. And they know instinctively how very often they are needed, which is an immense amount.

They are the fathers who—to use the verb form—*parent*; and they do this regardless of whether the relationship's origin was through the miracle of biology, a marriage blending individuals into a family, the gift of adoption, or merely as the result of a very unique friendship—because some bonds between people cannot be easily categorized.

They are the fathers we all know. The ones who have taken "Fatherhood" to heart. To these dads who so consistently love and support their children—and their children's mothers—we honor you.

MOMMY OUT OF CONTEXT

It's been said that the simplest questions are often the most profound. Such queries as *Who am I?* or *Where am I going?* top the list. And there are others like *What am I doing?* and *Where is my home?*

I've found myself thinking about all of those questions today—more so than usual. For today is a rare day: I'm spending it alone.

Who am I?

Usually I am "Mommy." Either "*MY* Mommy," according to my son, or "*HIS* Mommy," as referred to by my son's toddler friends and their parents. This was a disconcerting adjustment to make at first, having believed I'd earned a primary identity of my own—one not so completely tied to someone else's pronouns. Nevertheless, regardless of my former professional title as "classroom teacher" or my current one as "freelance writer," in the eyes of at least one important person in my life I have simply become "Mommy." I suspect, at some level, all mothers realize this.

That certain sense of being *possessed* by someone—being defined in relation to some other being—is hardly unique. As young girls we were *his* or *her* daughter, *their* niece, *his* cousin, or *her* granddaughter. We may have also been *his* or *her* sister, *his* wife/girlfriend/significant other, *her* best friend, and, eventually, *their* mother. When I taught full time I was, in the opinion of my students and even their parents, proprietarily referred to as *our* teacher.

But today it's just *me*, and only me. Stripped of the alternate identifiers, I find myself wading in a bit of selfhood murkiness. Without my son trailing behind me—or sprinting up ahead as an announcement—I'm left to present my own image to the world. It's an image I like.

Yet, even so, I'm overcome by the dispiriting sensation that what I'm projecting is an incomplete view. A vital part of who I am is not being represented. Can they tell? I ask myself this repeatedly. Can they figure out, from the odd aura of abandonment undoubtedly surrounding me, that I'm a mother let loose...out on her own without her child today?

No, I decide finally. Most cannot tell and probably do not care. Really, this feeling of the attached parent un-bonded for the day is of no importance to anyone but me. Not that I'm immersed in any activities worthy of extraordinary attention.

Where am I going? What am I doing?

Errands. I'm running errands. I do such things virtually every day: Returning library books or *Clifford* videos, stopping by the bank, picking up Q-tips and Kleenex from the neighborhood pharmacy, grabbing a head of lettuce and some chocolate soy milk at the grocery store, and so on. Uninspiring tasks, one might say. But what's unusual is for me to be doing them alone. The accustomed method is to navigate the interiors of adult buildings with all of the accoutrements a child requires. Strollers. Sippy cups. The ever-handy wipes. Small toys to provide distraction. Treats.

Wanderlust in Suburbia

And—oh, yes—keys, money, and my beloved library card. All the necessary passports.

Now I can just walk in and out unimpeded. I'm practically lost in adulthood. The librarian—someone who *does* know me—claims she nearly didn't recognize me today. I look different, she says. Oh, no, I think; it's apparent after all. I feel displaced even in this most familiar of settings. What am I forgetting? I ask this to my detached, movable self in panic. It all seems too easy. Too...too unencumbered.

But I do it anyway. I go through the motions—free from all responsibility to anything other than the task at hand. Traveling from one place to another—in straight lines even—without stopping to gape at the cement truck, without stomping curlicues in the snow with my boots, without tossing errant stones into the mud. I go in and out of the shop's revolving doors only once. And, then, I walk back.

Where is my home?

I enter with my bag of perceived necessities and encounter only silence. Hours remain before they're due to arrive; I still have the house to myself. The first few times this happened I collapsed, exhausted and in shock. Later, these periods gave way to precious moments of reflection, often accompanied by a massive mug of hot cocoa, which I would allow myself to drink slowly and without interruption. Sometimes I would find myself racing against the fast-moving minutes to complete required household chores, pay bills, or catch up on my correspondence. And a couple of times—I'll admit—I was like Tom Cruise's character in *Risky Business*: Dancing in carefree, teenager fashion to music from the oh-so-wild '80s. (Though only *very* rarely in my underwear.)

Today, I stop and stare at the emptiness. Home is usually here, but it is not yet here this afternoon. Not without my family, which for me now consists of my husband and our son. Can it be true that I am most myself, most sure of where I'm going and what I'm doing—and also most at home—when defined in relation to certain, very special others? Is this really the case, despite years of striving to be an accomplished individual in my own right? If so, then why does this realization not depress me? Or even mildly upset me?

Perhaps it's because I recognize that however much society may prize worldly accomplishment and perceived independence, we humans exist most happily within the bonds of love. That, in fact, without people we adore to share them with, the world's bounties feel hollow. Even when those bounties consist only of a new romantic comedy DVD and a bag of broccoli.

So here I am—floating like a lost electron—looking for the bonds I momentarily lack to complete the family molecule. The one I've come to feel is my home. My place of safely and where I can, most genuinely, be *me*. This is not a feeling attached to a building, a geographic spot, or a collection of objects, but a configuration of very specific individuals. The ones who make me cheerfully declare, "Home is where the heart is," and yet manage to keep me from thinking of it as a cliché.

Numerous variations on the configuration exist: Mom-Dad-Child(ren). Mom-Significant Other-Child(ren). Mom-Extended Family Members-Child(ren). Mom-Child(ren), etc. But being "Mom" is a central component for those of us so blessed with the title. Too central to camouflage from our souls for an afternoon or for an instant.

They return. My heart leaps to greet them.

Who are we? Where are we going? What are we doing? Where is our home? I ask these inaudibly to the two of them. They are simple questions, although undeniably profound. Somehow the answers to all have become entwined. Strands of togetherness, interdependence, love—strengthening us, pulling us closer, influencing who we are in relation to the others. Even after a day apart.

Or, maybe, especially then.

RAISING A "VERY ACTIVE" BOY

I'm not a "Girlie Girl." Really. I'm not. Sure, I had a few of those flouncy, lacy dresses in my closet that swished when you wore them and made you feel all princess-like when I was nine. And I owned my own Tang-orange Barbie Camper, like the ones everyone in the 1970s thought were so cool. And yeah, okay, I admit I adored my Easy-Bake Oven, even after we ran out of the nifty mix packets it came with...

But that was all kids' stuff.

It wasn't like I spent my study hall time daydreaming about future wedding china or bragging to my high school friends about how I'd inherit my grandmother's pearl necklaces and ruby rings someday. Nor, heaven forbid, did I waste even a moment's deep reflection on slight gradations in nail polish shades. At least not unless the occasion *really* warranted it. (It's rumored by some that I obsessed wildly about my fingernails the day before my wedding, but I refuse to substantiate such tales.)

My major claim to understanding the male psyche, of course, came from this single indisputable fact: I had a brother. Some people might require two or even three to get the full impact of Life With Men, but I was certain I needed only one. He was fascinating to watch. In a sentence, I learned from him that male children ran around a lot and broke things with alarming frequency. Not just ceramic plates, furniture, or their big sisters' art projects. No. But also their own arms, legs, and occasionally noses.

So I figured, when the ultrasound revealed we were having a baby boy, I might need to learn my way around the ER but, other than that, the chasm I'd have to bridge wouldn't be nearly so wide as it might for someone lacking my extensive knowledge. I was convinced my preparations were more than sufficient. And, anyway, when our son came on the scene he behaved, to my untrained eye, pretty much like every other baby—male or female—that we encountered out in public. This, I told myself, would be even easier than I thought.

Until he started walking or, rather, umm, sprinting. Store clerks, random patrons of the library, nurses, and our gentle pediatrician dubbed him a Very Active Boy. My friends with baby girls called me during "quiet play" time at their house, sharing endearing stories of how their sweet angels would curl up in their mommies' laps with no flailing limbs. How their little darlings would gaze peacefully at soft-fabric books for unfathomable stretches of time—like six entire minutes—or toddle cautiously around the edges of the sofa without once rocketing themselves at moving objects.

Meanwhile, my friends and I with similarly Very Active Boys installed deadbolts as we spoke on the phone, and had a few spare keys made for those inevitable moments when our precious sons accidentally locked us out of the house. (It happened to me twice before I took action.)

I should've been prepared. I knew what boys were

supposed to be like—that they were little destruct-o machines. Why didn't reality sink in? How could I let myself forget all the drawings my little brother shredded?

To answer my own question, it was because I was striving so hard NOT to be stereotypical. I remembered encountering some high-adventure-seeking little girls at the park. I also knew of a few boys who remained content to concentrate on a puzzle for a half hour without actually being chained to the spot. Diversity existed "out there," I was sure of it.

During college I'd spent countless hours studying culture and society and gender roles. I was convinced then—in a way you can only be when you're twenty and eating your meals out of a hotpot—that "environment" is virtually everything. That if my parents would've been socialized to accept and condone their *daughter* behaving like a whirling dervish in their living room (as opposed to their son who, twenty-five years later is shockingly more mild-mannered than their afore mentioned daughter), then I would've acquired stronger killer instincts, learned to speak a lot louder, and been altogether less huggy and nurturing than I am today.

Clearly, I'm not so sure of this anymore.

While I still believe environment is an immense, complex influence, I've come to be certain that male or female wiring takes precedence in many situations. And my informal poll of averages—that is, we parents with Very Active Boys—for reasons of self-esteem-preservation or simply day-to-day observation, lean heavily in the direction of "nature" when the debate arises.

And who would dare claim my son isn't huggy and nurturing, too? It often emerges in a delightful, spontaneous way with our son and with his friends. They hug, they share (sometimes), they take turns trying to bottle feed someone's baby sister, they're gentle with the dog or the pet newt. But usually this happens after they've managed to exhaust themselves running around the park for an hour, jumping on the trampoline, or climbing some piece of equipment that, to me, would've looked really high and dangerous when I was four.

Nevertheless, being as I am Not Quite a Girlie Girl who's raising a Very Active Boy, I confess to still having a lot of fun.

Despite the decimation of my Tupperware containers.

Despite the fear that my lovely glass music boxes won't survive to see the dawning of the New Year.

Despite the fact that it would take the impossible—catching my son and holding him down—to successfully comb his hair.

Despite all of the above, I'd trade my Barbie Camper and Easy-Bake Oven any day just to keep him a little (albeit Very Active) boy for just a tiny bit longer.

IN APPRECIATION OF GRANDPARENTS

We parents, by and large, get our fair share of attention and appreciation. Naturally, it's not nearly as much as we think we deserve, but when our kids thrive, well-wishers look to us to offer their congratulations. To applaud us for the role we played in our son's or daughter's success. Grandparents, on the other hand, are not always recognized as a shaping force in the lives of their children's children. But so many times that's exactly what they are.

My son, currently four-and-a-half years old going on forty, knows who to turn to when the chips are down or the spaghetti's cold.

"I really *love* Grandma," he declares to me, a mere onlooker, as a warm, heaping plate of his favorite food gets set down before him.

Grandma doesn't care about the mess he'll make. If she acknowledges it at all, the pleasure of watching him devour her Italian creation overrides the sauce stains on her pure white tablecloth. She's his cheerleader, his unshakable fan. Ever confident in his abilities. While nasty Mommy might criticize in the hopes of instilling some decent table manners

Wanderlust in Suburbia

in the distant future, my mother-in-law watches him dribble and splatter with only love in her gaze.

I'd be annoyed by her blindness if I weren't convinced that grandparents were gifted with a special kind of sight. A way of assessing the future character of loved ones two generations removed from them.

I wonder sometimes what my father-in-law sees when he looks at his only grandchild. As a World War II pilot and flight instructor, I know he's picked up on my son's love of airplanes. The two of them share a seemingly private understanding when it comes to kites, balloons, and other flying objects. When we encounter a new kind of airplane or when some pressing question about levitation arises, the common refrain is: "We'll have to ask Grandpa."

I think of all the worlds my young child has yet to discover. Will rockets fascinate him? Will he want to be an astronaut? He's already asking a million questions about outer space and our solar system. I'm always so thankful that he has someone in his life who is genuinely thrilled by the joys of flight. Someone who can share this love and wonderment with my baby boy.

My father shares different loves with his grandchild. As the "Out-of-State Grandpa," we aren't able to get together quite as often, but this doesn't stop my son from assigning certain specialties to my dad. This is the Grandpa who takes him to the zoo, sets up the backyard sprinkler for him on hot summer days, and knows how to garden. No words can express my elation and gratitude at having someone in the family who can keep plants alive long enough to teach our son about botany. Heaven knows, my husband and I kill every green thing we touch. My father saves space in his impeccable garden for his grandson's seedlings. The potted carrots and green beans that were wilting under my supervision get transplanted up in Wisconsin and, miraculously, grow into full, healthy and, yes, even edible plants.

If my son learns how to water vegetables and tend to living things, he didn't learn it from his parents. If he grows up to farm or to study agriculture, he got his first lessons as a preschooler—planting with Grandpa in June and "harvesting" in September.

And then there's my mother. Her role in her only grandchild's life is especially interesting to me because I remember so clearly when she was in *my* place. When she was the "Mommy" to a young, inquisitive child. I remember asking the endless questions that exasperated her. WHY this, WHY that. I remember my active brother running her ragged around the neighborhood. And now she has a grandson who does both. Is she annoyed and flustered by his queries? Worn out by his high-energy ways?

In a word, no.

I watched with amazement and mild horror as my son talked at her nonstop for hours while climbing on every piece of furniture within reach. When would her patience cease? When would she politely insist that we all go back to Illinois where we belong? It never happened. She, in fact, asked if he could stay the weekend. By himself. Without us there to protect her. Did he stay? Oh, yes, we would've been idiots to refuse such an offer. Did he have a marvelous time without boring old Mommy and Daddy? You bet. So much so that the kid was *angry* when we returned. He'd been having far too much fun with my parents and their friends, living it up as the center of attention. His request that my husband and I go away and leave him there for a whole week was not entirely surprising. My mother asking when he could come back again and if it could be soon...now *that* was a shock.

It's true, as the saying goes, "It takes a village to raise a child." Sometimes that village starts very close to home; sometimes it's separated by a little driving distance. But during September I'm always especially cognizant of four important members of my community, my village. September means many things to me: It's my birthday month, so I hope I'm getting wiser as well as older. As a former teacher, it's when school begins with freshness and optimism. My son's veggies will be ready to pick and, thus, a trip to a certain Wisconsin garden is on the agenda. And Grandparent's Day will be celebrated with extra enthusiasm in our house this year.

I know my husband and I can't take credit for our little boy's progress alone. I'm so thankful we have a few truly remarkable individuals by our side as he grows: Loving, involved grandparents who deserve honor and appreciation for all they've brought to our son's life.

FINGERPRINTS ON THE WINDOWPANE

A glance reveals a gray, smudged sight,
A gift by shaft of shining light,
Delivered to my waking eye
Though you no longer are nearby,
Your spirit's with me day and night.

Yesterday, captive by the rain,
With eyes glued to the windowpane,
You wished upon the glass somehow
And placed your hand in solemn vow,
Leaving behind your finger stain.

The wish was granted—you are gone,
A dancing child upon the lawn,
A morning bright, with friends you're out,
Free now to jump, run, climb, and shout,
Your joyous homage to the dawn.

Wanderlust in Suburbia

And I, inside, with thoughts of you,
Doing the work I need to do,
Put down my cloth and window spray…
I'll clean it off another day,
For now I'll just enjoy the view.

THE POWER OF GRATITUDE

1. Full moons.
2. Crunchy autumn leaves.
3. My husband.
4. Rock music from the '80s.
5. Loved ones' good health.
6. Chocolate of all varieties.
7. Compelling fiction.
8. Trustworthy friends.
9. Freedom.
10. My son's birthday.

Those are just a quick ten things I'm grateful for—the first set of many that spring to mind. Oh, I know they run the gamut from odd to commonplace to somewhat dignified, but I don't expect anyone else's list to mirror mine. People should be free to construct their own list and share it. Or not.

As for me, I've made a practice of giving thanks each night for treasures such as those. Even, sometimes, for the disappointments that get tossed my way, especially since I don't always recognize when I've encountered the proverbial "blessing in disguise." I've discovered that openly acknowledging my appreciation taps into an undeniable vein of power—a kind of warm reciprocation between the elements of good that exist and myself.

Admittedly, I still have difficulty pinning down the origin of that power—it's *source*. I wonder, does the process of saying "thank you" create such good karma that the positive forces of the universe join together to reward us with further blessings? Or, does the very act of seeking things for which to be thankful open our eyes to the true magnificence of our world and, thus, expand our awareness of what is available to appreciate? Is there another explanation?

I'm not sure.

But I've been told repeatedly by self-help writers, TV psychologists, and a variety of popular life coaches, etc., that consciously giving thanks for all we have in our lives is an act that changes us. That the more we express our gratitude, the more we'll have for which to be thankful.

An just about everyone suggests keeping a "gratitude journal"—a daily opportunity to jot down a few items we appreciate from the mundane to the profound.

Never one to leave blank spaces on anything (whether I had a worthy answer or not), I dutifully filled up my first gratitude journal with the requisite five things per day. Topping those early lists were entries that evidenced my obsession at the time—namely, striving for parenthood. On any given week, I might be thankful that my husband and I:

1. Passed our basic physicals.
2. Traveled together and experienced life as a couple beforehand.
3. Completed our graduate work.
4. Moved into a more accommodating, family-friendly living space.

5. Planned and saved accordingly for the still-mythic "Baby."

However, other fixations fought for recognition on the journal's pages. During those months I was almost equally thankful for:

1. Carryout pizza.
2. Musical theater.
3. Frequent-flyer miles.
4. A laser printer that worked.
5. My TV's unerring ability to record missed episodes of my favorite shows.

Treasures, I decided, came in many packages.

Some days, though, it was a struggle to come up with something new to appreciate. The umbrella stashed in the car on a rainy morning? Avoiding a traffic jam en route to the dentist? The new Szechwan place? True, I was learning to "see more" as time went on, but I was far from being fully observant.

Case-in-point: During pre-parenthood I was shockingly oblivious to such luxuries as an uninterrupted night's sleep, a dinner of adult-only food and conversation, or an evening of television blissfully free of *Blue's Clues* videos. I suppose I could say now that I'm grateful for the "perspective" life-with-toddler provides.

When we discovered I was expecting, I became instantly thankful for:

1. That little blue stripe.
2. The goddess known as my obstetrician.
3. Folic acid.
4. Mothers who had lots of personal survivor stories and tissues on hand.
5. Any opportunity to put my feet up.

Perhaps there are many people, parents or not, who are accustomed to being overwhelmed by the marvel of life, floored by the inherent responsibilities of true adulthood, and mesmerized by the blink of time's passing. People who possess far more natural perceptiveness than I had before my son's entry into the world. But I'm grateful now for those wise souls, too. Their presence helped me recognize what I was experiencing when baby-love knocked me over. All I knew then was that I was honored to get to be part of the motherhood adventure. And thankful—in advance—for all the lessons to come.

I remember being appreciative of every trimester that passed safely, of every doctor visit that ended uneventfully, and of every blood test that resulted in "normal." The more I was grateful for, the more I realized how much there was to say *thank you* for each night. Even when the ultrasound machine all but shouted "Beware!" and I was sent immediately to the hospital and placed in the high-risk ward, I was incredibly grateful for the skilled and speedy doctors, the top-of-the-line medical equipment, and the compassionate nursing staff. And for Shakespeare's immortal line, "All's well that ends well."

I do believe that expressing gratitude holds a special power, whatever its source. November is a time of year when citizens of our nation remind each other of our many blessings. Here at home, I have an additional, more personal reminder. Several years ago my son was born on Thanksgiving Day. For us, it's become a holiday entwined with strands of gratefulness, celebration of life, and a love of family. The miracle of his presence has, in fact, permeated every day of the year, forcing me to acknowledge that I can't confine my gratitude to merely the fourth Thursday in

November—even if it's become our family's biggest holiday.

I will, however, spend part of the night writing an especially long list of things I appreciate. I hope, whatever the size or style of your celebration, you and your loved ones will have extra-long lists, too.

THANKFULNESS AND EXPECTATIONS

During this time of year when we traditionally give thanks for our blessings, it occurred to me that I sometimes miss a good opportunity for gratitude, simply because my expectations are too steep, too unrealistic, too grandiose to recognize on first glance the worth of a subtler gift.

Take, for instance, "good health." We humans, by and large, tend not to fully appreciate the sheer magnificence of **not** having a cold, **not** having an ear infection, **not** having the flu or some other irritating malady until we experience its opposite. When my lower back aches, the world around me suddenly seems brimming with spine-crushing hazards and orthopedic obstacles. When I can't breathe through my congestion, the simple act of inhaling freely feels miraculous. In the days of recovery following my last muscle spasm or severe sore throat, I'm filled with thankfulness at being given relief from the pain or discomfort. But it doesn't take long for me to forget. To become consumed with different problems and to neglect to appreciate the absence of another.

In much the same way, it also falls into the realm of Human Nature to be dissatisfied financially. If we're still living with our parents, we want to be able to afford our own apartment. When we finally get that apartment, we want a more spacious one. Then we want to own the property. If it's a condo, we want a townhouse. If it's a townhouse, we want a single-family home. If it's a two-story, three-bedroom, nicely situated Colonial with curb appeal, we want an all-brick, six-bedroom McMansion on Lake Michigan. With our own moat and drawbridge. Oh, and a vacation home in Tuscany. And that's before we take into account all of the "extras" that go along with our elevated fantasy lifestyle: The designer clothes, the hot cars, the cool jewelry, the nifty holiday trips, and the upper-crusty restaurant reservations, and more.

Sarah Ban Breathnach, in her popular book **Simple Abundance**, refers to this problem and suggests we nurture a sense of "financial serenity" when such situations strike. In other words, to replace those internal messages of "I want this new material thing" with "I already have this important need." That our heartfelt appreciation for what we have now must come first. She writes of an ancient spiritual law, which basically states that the more you have and are grateful for, the more you'll be given.

I think Ban Breathnach is right. I know I, for one, have a tendency to hurry up and try to move onto the next level in something without stopping to acknowledge how far I've already come and to give thanks to the people who've helped me reach this point. Like little children, it seems that once we get a new toy or master a new task, we forget how long it took us to acquire or achieve it, how difficult doing whatever it was seemed to us at first. We forget that we didn't just jump out of our crib one day and begin racing down the hallway. (Well, my son came kind of close to doing that…) That we first had to learn to stand, then to balance with the help of some steady object or person, then to take that first step, fall down, get up again and again, then—finally—walk with confidence.

And, what's more, I think we're hardwired to have high expectations for ourselves. We're the heroes and heroines of our world, the stars of our own movies. And where our own egos fail, society steps in. We're bombarded with constant images, ones that confirm our belief that we need to look younger, thinner, stronger, wealthier, and more attractive. That we need to *be* better than those around us. Faster. Smarter. More powerful. So much so that tiny advancements are shrugged off as insignificant. That "progress" is considered worthy only when measured in leaps, not in tiptoes.

Thus, I'm reminding myself (and you) today, to take a step back from the daily chaos and give thanks for what is going well in our lives, right now—the large and the miniscule. To reign in those over-expectations and to, instead, appreciate every possession we've acquired and every tiny footstep we've taken in any area we've gained mastery: Our careers, our hobbies, our romantic relationships, our families and friends, our everythings.

Our paths may not always follow a straight line. In fact, any path worth taking rarely does. So, if it appears there are some reversals, backtracking, long pauses or whatever in our journeys, we should be thankful for those, too.

Elizabeth Gilbert, in her wonderful memoir **Eat, Pray, Love**, urges us to seek those things that bring us pleasure, not merely entertainment. A good meal. A beautiful view. The company of cherished friends. Such gifts are not only priceless treasures, but they often cost little, if anything.

And, so, in addition to the gifts I already have, I'm

inspired to look for one or two things today that fill my soul with happiness.

Seeing a bright-red cardinal on our birdfeeder.

Hearing a song I love on the radio.

Getting an unexpected hug from my son.

Eating ice cream, any flavor.

I will find them, enjoy them and give thanks for them—as, perhaps, you will, too—and I'll expect (with hope and gratitude) such continued blessings for all of us.

BLESSINGS AND INSANITY DURING THE HOLIDAYS

The Halloween costumes have long been packed away. The autumn leaves have been raked and disposed of properly. The leftovers from the Thanksgiving feast have been gobbled up and, at last, are really, truly gone from the refrigerator. We begin to delude ourselves into thinking that, after over two months of fall festivities, we deserve a break, a breather, a moment to look back on the preceding weeks of family-fun immersion with calm reflection and a sense of accomplishment.

Uh-huh. Think again.

The holidays are here. *Now.* And by golly we'd better get with the program 'cause it's later than we think. Some people began gearing up for this back in *September.* That's right. They know who they are...but they're not us. We're the ones who are *behind.* The ones who put off thinking about this month because revving up the ole holiday spirit is more difficult when we're too frazzled to breathe. Everywhere we look we're reminded that it's only (fill in the number) more shopping days until (fill in the holiday). It doesn't matter which specific December event we celebrate. This time of year is a non-denominational, equal-opportunity, high-stress month regardless. And don't even think of trying to get out of it. What would your (fill in the relative) say?

I made the mistake of going mall shopping with my preschooler the day after Halloween. We watched as store employees gleefully replaced the orange and black with a tidal wave of red and green. There were blue and white splashes down the aisles, too. And ribbons and wrapping paper everywhere.

My son's grin broadened with each snow globe we passed, every stocking set out for purchase. I could almost see him envisioning dancing sugarplums and a truckload of superhero action figures in his little Disney-loving head.

"Is it almost Christmas, Mommy?" he asked, beaming at the sheer magnitude of breakable display items.

"NO!" I shouted back. But the bags of candy canes, racks of Santa hats, and rows of tree ornaments belied my interjection.

And why wouldn't he believe them over me? As the clock ticked down the minutes of November, the shops became increasingly more, um, merry. Colored lights started flashing. In-store commercials grew louder and more insistent. Holiday tunes could not be ignored. They were piped in through overhead speakers—played as repetitively as if they contained subliminal messages to buy, buy, buy, shop, shop, shop—all to the jiving Musak melody of "Winter Wonderland." People get depressed and dream of jumping off (fill in a high place) during this time of year for a reason.

Oh, we know commercialism is rampant all the time, but especially during the holidays. Most people accept this as a given. And, to further fuel this drive, we're reminded annually of Marley's warnings to Scrooge to be kind and generous to others. We don't need three ghosts haunting us to get the message that we'd better be on our best behavior and be ready to pull out our MasterCard at a moment's notice.

Yet, it isn't for lack of caring or generosity toward our friends, loved ones, or even indifferent acquaintances that make us want to cower under our snowflake comforter. It's just that December can be so overwhelming. And the expectations so steep. And the month-plus of work and anticipation rarely competes with the reality. I usually don't feel fully recovered from the festivities until well after New Year's, and the Post-Holiday Slump plagues most of my friends and family as well.

I'd like to think that (fill in the year) could end the way I imagine it. It's a decades-old fantasy. The one where I'm the epitome of balance and perspective. The one where I sagely do not repeat past years' mistakes. The one where I'm finally able to sift through the chaos and fruitcake and focus instead on the heart of the holidays. The year comes to a close with a swell of "Auld Lang Syne." A feeling of peace, light as angels' wings, settles on my soul.

I keep assuring myself it can be done. Yet, just like my every-year New Year's resolution to lose those ten—okay, *twenty* pounds, I find myself stumbling over the same (fill in the pitfall), holiday after holiday, disappointed that I'd expected too much and wishing I could do it all better.

So, what can we do? How can we stay sane and keep the true spirit of giving and sharing alive amidst the barrage of commercials and last-minute-shopper super sales? How do we remember to count our blessings on days when the demanding nature of "the season" threatens to shred our good will toward men/women/anyone?

I'm not the right person to offer an easy answer, but I do think a kind of solution exists. I suspect it has something to do with tapping into that elusive but oft-desired sense of balance and perspective, even if it's only for a few random minutes between gift-wrapping packages.

Some people meditate. Some pray. I know I've touched that sensation of peacefulness when my child is snuggled in my arms, the flashing colored bulbs reflected in his excited brown eyes. I've heard it when a finger-snapping carol breaks through one of my minutes of "Bah, Humbug!" discontent, and I find myself humming, smiling, and greeting passersby with the warm feelings of kinship possible when our hearts are open. I might even go so far as to say I've smelled and tasted it when my mom offers us a plate of scrumptious cookies she made especially for our visit.

The spirit of the holidays is sprinkled on these moments. And, these days, when I encounter them, I've learned to cherish them for as long as they last. Getting caught up in the frenzy is easy; I've been trying not to be so hard on myself when this happens.

But when I can remember to step back, I'm likewise reminded that the true gifts are those we don't need to tie bows onto and don't have to worry about somebody returning. They're the joy we have in each other's company, the preciousness of the time we share, the rare but wonderful instances of magic.

So, whenever possible, hold tight to what you find you're grateful for during the holidays. Spread cheer around when you can. Don't get down on yourself when you can't. And I'd add this—bless you, (fill in your name), and your family. Or, in the immortal words of Tiny Tim, "God bless us, every one."

And we'll need all of those blessings because the holidays are here. *Now.*

THE BEST HOLIDAY GIFTS EVER

Every year around this time, I tell myself I'm not going to flip out when those obnoxious commercials come on TV. You know the ones I mean. They've got insanely cheerful actors from Company A dancing onscreen to jingly music in little Santa outfits while Potential Gifts for Everyone on Your Holiday Shopping List flash before your eyes in thirty-second intervals. Then Companies B, C, and D have their turns, and pretty soon you feel as though your irises are pulsing out of your head like a Looney Toons character.

Yeah, we've all been there.

When faced with such exposure to conspicuous consumption, it's easy to delve into depressing laments about the commercialism of the holidays, the materialistic trends of our society in general, or any number of topics that only leave me wanting to devour batches of sugar cookies (made fresh by Company E) for comfort. So I won't do that.

Instead, I'm reminded of five of the best holiday gifts I've ever been given. I'll share them with you, although you should know upfront that none of them came from Companies A through E.

1. ***Encouraging Parents.*** When I was four, I was cast as an Unnamed Elf in my preschool's production of "A Christmas Program." (Okay, that may not be quite the right title, but it was something like that.) It wasn't a big part. My "elf" had a total of one or two lines of dialogue, and I spent most of the show standing stage right, trying to look "festive"…but I was so proud of my role. I was clad, appropriate to the season, in a red knit dress with white tights, so I looked more like a chunky candy cane than one of Santa's helpers, but I didn't care. As far as I was concerned I was glamorous. The star of the show. My parents had taken off of work to see me perform in my first dramatic role, and they couldn't have made me feel more special about the whole experience. And, though I lack the acting talent to make a habit of being onstage myself, my love of "theater" began that very afternoon and, since then, it's brought me decades of joy.

2. ***Letting Go.*** Fast forward several years and I was in high school. I wanted very much to become an AFS exchange student. Not because I thought it would distinguish me in the eyes of college admissions boards, or anything that strategic, but just because I wanted to go somewhere, *anywhere*, else. What were a few thousand miles when the world was so vast and so foreign? Who wanted to stay in the Midwest their whole lives—or so I wondered at age sixteen? That winter break, my parents, with worry in their eyes, said, "Yeah, go ahead and apply." Now, as a parent myself, I know they were probably hoping I'd get turned down flat and would, consequently, cease all of this nonsense about leaving the country. Their gift to me was their willingness to let me try and, if necessary, to let me go. (Which was what happened. Six months later, they let me take a nine-thousand-mile trip to

Australia…)

3. *A Fresh Perspective.* Few gifts really top motherhood, especially in the very beginning when every day is counted with amazement. Falling asleep with my 28-day-old newborn beside me for our first Christmas Eve together felt magical. It was as though all I finally *heard* all of those carols I'd grown up singing. The lyrics to "Silent Night" spoke to me in a new way, and I hummed the melodies of all my favorites, blessing my son. I wore a thick, floor-length red and green flannel robe for pretty much the entire month of December. It didn't matter that I looked truly hideous in it (far worse, even, than in the candy-cane elf outfit); its warmth comforted my baby, and me as well. He snuggled up next to me—a tiny, squirmy bundle of love—and I watched him watch the colored lights blinking and the snow falling before he drifted back to sleep.

4. *A Supportive Husband.* A few winters ago, I got this strange notion that writing full time would be "a great new career path." Looking back on that decision, my husband probably should've responded with healthy skepticism and an in-depth analysis of my mental state. Instead, when I told him I wanted to learn more about writing professionally, he listened and smiled. And when I explained I was considering taking a class at a nearby university, maybe, in the summer or sometime…he interrupted me and said, "Why wait? Enroll now. You could start in January!" Living with a man who has that kind of faith in me is a true gift, and it's a great combatant of fear. I think we all need to have someone in our life who says with conviction, "You can do it." Someone we know who really believes this, especially on days when we don't believe.

5. *Feeling Safe.* Tonight, as I look outside at the dark, chilly sky, I'm grateful for getting to stay home and still feel

secure. I know that out there in the world our brave troops are protecting us at great risk to themselves and great sacrifice to their families. I'm aware of what a privilege it is to live in this extraordinary country, despite its faults and regardless of where we as individuals lie on the political spectrum. And I think we're tremendously fortunate to have intelligent soldiers defending our nation—men and women who've made it their jobs to help the rest of us feel safe.

Remembering these treasured gifts from past and present helps me keep the holiday-buying craze in perspective. Sure, there are many people on my "shopping list" who might want something from Company A or B, etc. but, hopefully, they'll appreciate other, less tangible gifts, too. Because, in the opinion of someone who was once the Happiest Unnamed Elf in the Midwest, those are the best kind.

SNEAKING UP ON THE HOLIDAYS

Almost every year the holidays sneak up on me. The days and weeks leading up to them pass in a blur of seasonal landscape and, like the sudden appearance of Santa's Headquarters at the northbound end of *The Polar Express* ride, Christmas-Hanukkah-Kwanzaa-etc. materialize just as abruptly at the conclusion of my yearly journey.

It's not that I'm not expecting them, mind you. It's just that I tend to forget (due to self preservation? selective amnesia? too many Snickers miniatures in late October?) that the pressure can get heaped upon us so quickly, so dramatically. That once we've made it passed the wilds and horrors of Halloween, it's open season for paralyzing self-doubt, unrealistic family expectations, and rampant consumerism, all sung to the chipper tune of "It's the Most Wonderful Time of the Year." The whole thing usually makes me a tense, irritated, and distressingly pessimistic writer.

Only, that's not the way it went down for me, at least not this year. THIS year I wasn't blindsided. THIS year I saw the holidays coming, although, admittedly, I'm not sure what accounted for it. (I'm currently blaming my enhanced vision and the holidays' more pronounced visibility on that bizarre, too-early snowfall in the first week of October.) But, regardless, I witnessed their approach...and it gave me the gift of a fresh perspective.

I guess, having the unanticipated luxury of preplanning for the first time in decades, I wasn't quite so engulfed in the usual Holiday Preparation Chaos come December. Unlike every other year since I became an "official" (i.e., self-supporting) adult, I began my holiday shopping early. This very act transformed me into one of those obnoxious people we all resent. You know the ones. Those overly industrious souls who brag about how they bought their presents in the first few weeks of fall, when stores were still comparatively uncrowded and the salespeople were still unharried and eager to help them in the maniacal hunt for Toys, Electronics, or Housewares.

So, when I say I was done with my shopping by Veterans Day (don't hate me for this—I already admitted it was insufferable behavior), you can understand the time I had on my hands. With the notable exception of a hectic Thanksgiving weekend, I was granted about six uninterrupted weeks to partake in activities like holiday home decorating, cookie baking, and gift wrapping. Having neither a natural talent in, nor a great personal affinity for, doing much of any of these, I turned my attention to my favorite pastime—people watching/blatant eavesdropping—and to a rare attempt at getting *into* the "spirit" of the season, as opposed to merely being besieged *by* it.

Nifty, heartwarming stuff started happening.

The airwaves were, as usual, abuzz with the Songs of the Season and, although the cynic in me got a tad edgy when I heard Christmas carols being played mere hours after

Halloween ended, I soon found myself enjoying them, making time to listen to my favorites and even singing along. The tunes inevitably called to mind Christmases past, and I caught myself reminiscing about holidays I'd shared with my parents/brother/other relatives in the years before my husband and son came on the scene and, of course, afterward, too.

But, besides the pleasure of remembered celebrations, I daydreamed about future ones, imagining what Christmas with my son might be like when he turned 14 or 22 or 37... I studied the faces of people currently at those ages, watching their expressions, which tended to range from delighted youthful exuberance to frenzied adult exhaustion. I wondered what it would take to help my son retain a bit of his age-8 enthusiasm, even three or four decades later. I, likewise, wondered why it had been so hard for me to do the same. Could this annual tradition of "feeling overwhelmed" be the only thing keeping me from experiencing the simplest and most basic joys of the Season?

Curiosity over this question and, well, stubbornness, motivated me to put a little more effort into the holidays, to want to make them even more celebratory. No, I still didn't go all out on the home décor/baking thing, but I focused on fairly uncomplicated details. I made time to do a few festive tasks I'd skimmed over or avoided in recent years: Making a batch of frosted Christmas cookies. Cutting out paper snowflakes. Even constructing a gingerbread house (from a kit, you guys, not from scratch—I didn't have *that* much time). These reminded me of a range of goofy things I used to do with my college roommates and, later, with my classes of 2nd and 3rd graders. And, oddly, it was as if participating in those very activities created a way for me to turn the tables and sneak up on the holidays, instead of vice versa. To recapture, on *my* terms, a bit of that Christmassy cheer and liveliness I so admired in others but feared I'd lost myself.

I realized what I was craving most was a positive holiday attitude accompanied by a sense of control. That my wintertime feelings of being a Helpless Snowflake in the Fatal Path of the Snowplow of Life not only made for a dreadful metaphor but a pretty pathetic way of living through the holiday season. So, I decided to look for other ways to reclaim my December. Ways to join in the merriness without being bulldozed by it.

The first was to "just say no" to too much sociability. I needed to choose my battles or, rather, my social gatherings carefully. I couldn't attend everything and trying to do so would've made me as crazed as I'd been in prior years. I figured my true friends would understand that I couldn't go to every event. (A belief that proved happily true.)

The second was to downplay the materialistic side of the Season. Granted, this was easier to do because I wasn't actively shopping anymore, but I avoided malls the way I avoided stale slabs of fruitcake. It also helped when I could flick off the TV or radio (and with them those relentless commercials) and put on a fun DVD or CD instead.

Third, I thought about charitable giving and which causes I could make a priority this year. For those who can afford grand gestures of generosity, that's great, but being able to contribute even a little extra time, money, or service to something you value (like your place of worship; neighborhood mainstays like your local library/community center/YMCA; a food pantry; or helpful organizations such as the Red Cross/United Way/Salvation Army) is priceless. The key for me was to be able to give consciously—not to blindly toss some change into a jar when cornered at the grocery store—but to choose deliberately and meaningfully what I most wanted to support this year.

Finally, taking time off to do a few things I really loved—and not feeling guilty about it—has been a sanity saver. For some this might mean participating in winter sports or attending riotous parties. For me, it's reading novels late into the night that aren't on my book-reviewing list, getting to drink enormous mugs of hot cocoa laced with peppermint, playing music as a family, and watching the snow falling or the colored lights flashing from our window as darkness overtakes the sky.

All in all, it's not a bad way to sneak up on the holidays…and, in my most optimistic moments, it's a way to embrace them.

ONE ROTATION

Baby
Morning Angel
Thumping, Babbling, Observing
Daytime Explorer
Child
Afternoon Angst
Standing, Kicking, Chewing
Peaceful Evening
Dreamer.

RESOLVING TO DO SOMETHING "BIG"

The tinsel is packed away again. The photo-greeting cards have been pulled off the refrigerator. You've devoured your very last candy cane of the season, and you swear if another cookie came along it would have to bite into you before you'd bite into it. With the usual resolution to lose those holiday pounds still ringing in your ears, you look at the untouched calendar in front of you, flip it open to January and wonder: Will I accomplish this year's goals?

Well, at least that's what I always do.

I've made the "I'm Gonna Lose Ten (or Fifteen or Twenty…) Pounds This Year *For Sure*" vow ever since New Year's 1983. And the end result will be, this time, really spectacular. I'll be amazingly trimmed and toned. A model of health and fitness. A walking ad for the power of daily exercise and fresh water consumption. Yep, that's me, Ms. Aerobic Step-n-Spin of the 21st Century.

Unfortunately, except for a very successful—but, alas, very brief—weight-loss stint back in the early '90s, I haven't veered far from this standby resolution because I, um, haven't yet achieved it to my satisfaction.

But what would I resolve to do with the coming year if I weren't determined to fit into that cute navy pencil skirt I once wore pre-pregnancy? Hmm. Work on world peace?

A great idea, really, but seriously…what could *I* do? Me. Wife, mother, northern Illinois resident, freelance and fiction writer, pretty average woman in her mid-thirties. Let me reiterate: Not a movie star. Not a politician. Not a wealthy, well-connected socialite.

The problem is, even with my clear lack of international relations skills, the idea of striving toward some large-scale goal keeps haunting me. I don't know why precisely. It isn't as though I have a lot of globally involved role models out there in my fruit-snack-toting, mom-of-a-preschooler world. Not many of us can make time for any "big causes" beyond chauffeuring the munchkins to class and keeping them from strangling each other at playgroup. (Although maybe, in this small way, we *are* working toward world peace.)

For me, perhaps, this determination to make a major change of some kind on New Year's morning has to do with an idealism from long ago that never dissipated. An age-old desire to do something "significant," like helping to achieve harmony in the Middle East. Or, maybe, discovering a cure for cancer, the common cold, AIDS, or this nasty flu that's been going around. Or, somehow solving the food and water shortage so no human will be without.

I don't dream of doing trivial things, like finally cleaning out my kitchen cabinets and recycling all the unused plastic bags stashed inside. Oh, no. I want the feeling that I'm contributing to a global good in a way that is obvious and important. Events I can point to for the rest of the year (perhaps even for the rest of my life) to remind myself that I made a "real difference" somehow, somewhere.

Unfortunately, since I know nothing about medicine, agriculture, or politics, I'll have to be content with lesser vows.

Yet, this makes me wonder why, when I make those yearly resolutions, I still insist upon them being so dramatic? Why can't I be satisfied with a small change over the course of the year? One small, personally significant change? Why, in order to feel a sense of accomplishment, would I need a United Nations badge or, at the very least, the crew from "Extreme Makeover"?

As in all things, I suppose, I need to seek a sense of balance and perspective with this. I spent an inordinate amount of time trying to stay in touch with those two concepts before the holidays. Now, post-holiday, I need them even more. I am a wife, a mom, a northern Illinois resident with skills in education, psychology, writing and cooking (especially meals containing disguised vegetables). These skills may not be enough to put an end to civil unrest in Africa, but they're not worthless either.

I have friends who, while not able to solve world hunger single-handedly, still help out at a soup kitchen for a couple of hours a month. Others who, though unable to stamp out all illiteracy, volunteer each week to teach basic reading to kids and adults. Family members who organize events for the Special Olympics. A wonderful writing organization I belong to that used to sponsor an annual book sale on Valentine's Day weekend called "All For Love" with the proceeds going to the American Heart Association. People everywhere, everyday are involved in activities that appear miniscule at first glance and, yet, they benefit others and make our world a better place.

No one doubts this. Everyone needs this kind of help.

And most people acknowledge these tiny tasks we take on with open arms and grateful hearts. Sometimes I wish I could remember to do the same when it comes to my more mundane daily life. I wish I'd remember to pat myself and my friends and family members on the back for the small but necessary things we do for ourselves and for each other throughout the year. These activities may not be huge, but they are important nonetheless.

Likewise, my latest New Year's resolution need not be something spectacular, just something meaningful and important, however small. Maybe just promising to make healthy, wholesome meals for my family. Or, making sure we get enough rest and fresh air and exercise. That...and losing those last few pounds.

ON BEING EXTRAORDINARY IN AN ORDINARY LIFE

I once read a fascinating blog post on the subject of normalcy. The author was explaining how dissatisfying it can be to live a so-called "normal" life, especially when we crave to be seen as special. How an ordinary, non-celebrity-like existence can trap us into feeling distressingly average.

This is a frustration I understand all too well.

Thanks to healthy childhood egos, most of us are born believing the universe revolves around us (or, at least, it *would*, if the universe knew what was best for it). Once we're older and have finally gotten over the pain of this misinterpretation, we step into adolescence. Now we're convinced that even though the world may not bow to our every whim or machination, everybody in it is still watching us, analyzing our actions, unduly curious about our motivations. And a few people really are: Our parents, primarily, and our Great-Aunt Charlotte in Dubuque.

Most people, however, are caught up in their own dramas—real or self-created—and the audience we believed to be tracking our every move is, in fact, imaginary. (Refer to those pervasive Psych 101 textbooks foisted annually upon college freshmen; there's always some chapter on teenage delusion and "the imaginary audience," trust me.)

But, as traumatic as it may have been to come to terms with the universe's failure to act upon our commandments, it's even worse when we discover as adults that, all too often, it hasn't even noticed us. The result is that we feel ineffective, invisible and—most troubling of all—insignificant. What can we do to combat this? Short of taking up X-treme Sports or following in the hallowed footsteps of Mother Teresa, what can make us feel that we're alive, unique, and/or contributing something valuable to humanity?

Many profess that a strong relationship with a Higher Spiritual Power is the answer. While I couldn't begin to explore this topic as extensively as it deserves, I'll go far enough out on a limb to say that getting in touch with one's spiritual side, if, indeed, one is inclined to attempt it, couldn't hurt. Entertainers, sports figures, and creative artists in every field profess their gratitude to whichever God they honor (as noted by their CD-insert thank-you messages, their Oscar acceptance speeches, and their post-contract-signing press conferences). To have a healthy spiritual relationship in which guidance is obtained and wisdom is derived may well bring with it some reassurance, some sensation of being on The Right Track, whatever that track might be.

Another tactic, often employed, is that of self-discovery journals and writing exercises. Jotting down the thoughts, emotions, questions, etc. that bubble to the surface after participating in an experience designed to elicit reflection could, likewise, give an individual some much-needed personal insight. Might these ruminations lead to a greater understanding of who we are, where we're going, what we really want out of life? Perhaps. Again, it's hard to believe trying it could hurt.

How about reading inspiring works of literature? Or participating in acts of charity? Or supporting what you believe are positive causes, be they social, religious, or political in nature? Why not, I say. Give 'em a go. I wish there were clear, well-marked paths that would bestow every individual with the assurance of fulfillment in this lifetime. Perhaps a person far wiser than I am would know just where to look.

Some may argue that we are, simply by virtue of being human, already pretty extraordinary. Others may claim that merely behaving in an honorable, hardworking, and honest manner is plenty unusual. But, while I'm inclined to agree with both statements to a degree, I also know that these two forms of defying one's fear of averageness are rarely enough. Most people want something *more*. Day-to-day living, even if it's honest work, etc., can seem so colorless and tedious next to the glamour of a celebrity's lifestyle. And it's not only the money and fame that seduces us. In many cases, it's the actor's/musician's/sports-hero's sheer talent and the world's overt recognition of it.

For my part, there's only one thing I'm remotely confident about suggesting. It's that, whether you're already a household name or not, there are few, if any, shortcuts to greatness. That whatever method you use to try to find your Best Self, it doesn't happen instantaneously or effortlessly. (No, not even for *American Idol* finalists or Oprah Book Club authors.) Most of us don't get Big Breaks—the lottery win so we can quit our day job to paint watercolors in Florence, or the talent agent who discovers us singing "The Greatest Love of All" on karaoke night downtown. Name your fantasy. We get, maybe, modest opportunities that pop up, if we're prepared enough to recognize them and willing to do the work they require.

Becoming someone "extraordinary" appears to be an almost endless process of learning and changing and dealing with whatever you have to confront in order to be the person you envision. This, and a commitment to excellence in your chosen arena that probably borders on obsession. I suspect the frustrations we have with our perceived ordinariness largely stem from wanting to rack up a series of impressive accomplishments or esteemed qualities before we've had a chance to earn them.

I've certainly been guilty of this.

What parent doesn't want to be known as The Best Mom or Dad Ever? Yet, a child's character is built little by little, in tiny increments over the years, and it's a rare day during those first couple of decades when we feel we've gotten it all right. Will my son nominate me for Mother of the Year when he's 18? I don't know. (If his fury at me this weekend was any indication, I doubt it.) But, until time has a chance to prove my superior judgment on the subject of _____ (fill in major parent-child argument), I'm just your average, ordinary mom, doing my best at this often rewarding, sometimes boring, and always unpredictable parenting gig.

And what person doesn't want to be thinner and fitter with less effort? (Have the motivations behind those New Year's Resolutions waned for anyone else yet?) What professional doesn't want to have his or her career goals fall into place, as if by a genii's decree? Or to get the coveted raises/promotions/accolades/respect we all hope are coming to us? Who wouldn't want to be thrilled every time they glanced at their checking-account balance? Or overwhelmingly happy in their significant relationships? Or a frontrunner in any endeavor the world collectively regards as highly prized?

I guess the drive to become extraordinary in anything requires—above all—courage. The courage to suffer through being achingly average, normal, ordinary in some field until you can build up the skills needed to reach the exalted heights you've aspired to. The courage to follow the small, mundane steps that are prerequisites to attaining that next level. And what many of us forget in our daydreams of grandeur is that there'll always be another Everest to climb. That whatever it is that makes you feel as though you've scaled a mountain and earned that rush of achievement today will feel downright commonplace tomorrow…leaving you to seek a new challenge elsewhere.

Moreover, what we may fantasize as an extraordinary life is, to someone else, their typical day, full of frustrations and petty annoyances. Alternately, what we're so often convinced is our own bland normalcy is, to another person out there somewhere, the absolute vision of remarkableness and accomplishment. So, while hard work is always the constant, the level of perceived success remains relative.

English essayist and critic John Ruskin once wrote, "The highest reward for a person's toil is not what they get for it, but what they become by it." To paraphrase a bit of Thoreau's wisdom here, too: Go ahead and build your castles in the air—that's where those dreams and ambitions belong and begin—but don't neglect to put foundations under them.

Finding our passion and dreaming big dreams…making a commitment to pursuing what we love then following through…what could be more inspiring and less ordinary than that?

SPRING CLEANING

The words "spring cleaning" have taken on a whole new significance for me this year because this spring—this month, in fact—we're moving. From the moment we were officially "under contract," I was forced to do something I'd been dreading for a full seven years: slide open our junk closet door all the way. I had to peer inside, to be brave as I watched numerous familiar but long-ago-misplaced objects tumble out...and yet I had to refrain from slamming the door shut and avoiding the responsibility that awaited inside. The task before me was more substantial than it initially appeared. I was, in essence, required to confront my past, see it anew with my present eyes, and decide if its symbols (all stuffed haphazardly in bags or boxes) had any place in my future. Is it any wonder trepidation came marching in?

I pulled out the easiest items first—the ones I knew were nonnegotiable "keepers." I was certain the film negatives from the 104 rolls of film we'd taken since our son's birth five years ago would be coming with us. (No exaggeration on the number of rolls, by the way. I had the packages numbered.) It was also a no-brainer to hang onto the extra blankets and pillows we'd kept stashed in this closet. A mom can never have too many bedding items on hand, and the new house will have a bit more space, enough for a guest bedroom. Since our young one's swimming ability is still somewhat tenuous, the orange water wings were transferred to a moving box. So were my husband's winter sweaters. And, for obvious reasons, the still-working 35mm camera.

Then came the things that were easy to toss: The crinkled tidbits of wrapping paper, several worn plastic toys we thought we'd fix but that'd stayed broken for months instead, my least favorite Halloween witch's hat and cape. I was pleased with myself, at least on the short term, for going against my packrat tendencies and finally filling up those garbage bags.

But, alas, the challenge came. My personal Waterloo. The items that didn't fit neatly into either of the previous categories had to be examined and choices had to be made. There were books from graduate school I hadn't looked at in eons. Fascinating stuff, but was it applicable to my life now? And what to do with our son's first set of baby clothes? The "0-3 Months" outfits I hadn't been able to part with before? Those tiny little shirts and pants pulled at my heartstrings and filled my mind with the hazy, happy memories of those early days of motherhood. And then there were my pregnancy dresses. I swore I'd never, EVER wear them again, yet the patterns of those fabrics haunt me still. They were part of an era that passed, and looking at them today makes me all sentimental and weepy, even though the era we're in now is a good one.

When pressed to explain, I suppose my dilemma stems from viewing certain objects as symbols or relics. When such little treasures are set before me, the decision to keep one means that I've deemed the memory associated with the given object as something I "cherish." When I give it away or toss it out instead, I feel I've branded the memory "unimportant" somehow. And how could any memory involving our child, the forty-two-inch Light Of Our Lives, be unimportant?

Well, I've concluded that the memory isn't inconsequential, but that holding onto a symbol you've outgrown is something you must approach with caution. If the object is kept as a marker of how far you've come—in other words, a measurement of growth—then I believe it's a healthy thing in moderation. However, if the object is a reminder of a path long ended and you've yet to embark on a new one, perhaps those relics need to be let go and your ties to them set free—so you have room, both physical and emotional space, for your new passions to fill. At least that's what I told myself as I dropped many of my dusty grad-school books in the library's donation box.

But I also kept a few, my very favorites, to stand on the bookshelf next to my current stash of page-turners. Not everything from those days is irrelevant, and for that I'm grateful.

I got rid of all but my most memorable, my most *floral* pregnancy dress. It makes me grin to look at it—yards upon yards of unflattering fabric. Big enough to fashion a springtime tablecloth, should I be so inclined. (Not that I'd ever really do it, but the thought continues to amuse me…)

As for my son's infant outfits, I kept them. Every one. Well, okay, not the stained, no-longer-white sleeper—but all the others from that very early period. We *have* come a long way since then, and mere photos of these particular symbols don't do them justice. They're a record of his growth (mine, too, as a mom), and I'd be happy to relinquish them someday, but only to our son himself.

Or, maybe, to his baby boy.

We're moving just a twenty-five-minute drive away, but there's a mental distance we're creating, an era we're leaving behind. As I clean our house in preparation for departure, I want to take with me only the very best of this time. All in all, I think I have.

OUR OWN DRUMMERS

Several springs ago, when my son was just a baby, I asked myself a series of predictable new-mommy questions. The top three were:
1. Isn't he an amazing, miraculous creature?
2. How on earth am I going to take care of him?
3. Will I *ever* lose this extra weight?

Once I'd survived the initial hazy months of motherhood, I was certain of the answer to the first question, and my confidence and skill level were growing in response to the second...but what to do about the third remained a constant concern.

I stared out our kitchen window. The frosty winter was finally behind us, birds beckoned each other with calls of love, and the tulips in the neighbor's flower garden held the promise of a delightful spring. No more excuses.

I unearthed my Nikes from the overflowing hallway closet, only to find that my feet were no longer a size 7 ½. Pregnancy, it seemed, permanently swelled more than just my fat cells. The next week, and a trip to our nearest shoe store later, I was ready. Really ready. I strapped my darling four-month-old into his stroller, swaddled him lovingly in three fuzzy blue blankets, stashed a bulging tote bag (filled with only the most essential baby items) in the underneath basket, and headed out into the day. Naptime was over. It was now time for fitness, and we were going walking.

I loved it. The joy of introducing my baby to the natural wonders surrounding us, conversing with him, singing silly songs—these were all endlessly fascinating, at first. His interest lasted about two weeks, my voice even less. As a fairly quiet person by nature, I'd been spending the majority of my time at home going against type—jabbering to him about moons and caterpillars and things so as to ensure he received enough verbal stimulation. By the time we got outside, we both needed a break. I wanted to exercise my muscles not my vocal cords, and I had a great desire to put some swing into my step. Headphones, I decided, were the solution.

I made compilation tapes of my favorite fast-tempo pop hits of the '80s. I found and dusted off my ancient Walkman. Baby Boy slept to the gentle rocking of the stroller while I walked to the beat of The Go-Go's. Exercise had never been so blissful, and I never had a reason to expect this might change. As a child, I'd loved being pushed in the stroller, getting to watch the world go by while someone else expended the energy. Why, I asked myself, would our son be any different? He was, after all, *my* child. I was certain I had years of cardio health in front of me with this method of fitness.

Well, not quite.

Babyhood gave way to toddlerhood. During his time of transformation, I managed to shed many (although, sadly, not all) of the pounds I'd so gleefully gained when I was pregnant. And, as our little one went from crawling to walking to sprinting, I took him to parks further and further away, armed with Goldfish and Juicy Juice.

Then, disaster struck.

"No! No walk, Mama!"

He was two years old, jealous of my Walkman, antsy, contrary, and increasingly verbal. Maybe, I realized too late, I shouldn't have talked to him quite so much when he was an infant.

"But we'll get to go to that nice park you like," I pleaded. "The one with that big climbing thing."

"No!" he screamed, fondling my Walkman and glaring at me with well-practiced toddler fury. I saw him try to put the headphones over his ears. Backwards.

"What if I let you listen to some music on the way?"

He looked interested. Ah, I thought, my burgeoning little Mozart!

Only, he seemed to prefer the alternative sounds of new millennium rock, classic Carole King, anything from the *Dragon Tales* soundtrack, and the full-length cast recording of *Joseph and the Amazing Technicolor Dreamcoat*. I didn't ask questions. Within a week, I'd given him my Walkman (I had a handheld CD player that I could use), made a bunch of cassette tapes to keep him entertained, and expanded my basket of supplies to include emergency AA batteries.

Once we took to the sidewalk, we received some pretty comical looks from passersby. With both of us wearing our individual headphones and swinging to different beats (my son rocking 'n' rolling in the stroller and me pushing it from behind), the expressions we encountered ranged from amused to confused to curious. But it was fun and, even more importantly, it worked. My level of aerobic fitness continued to climb, and he got a shot of musical education on the yellow brick road to the park.

His musical tastes grew as he did and, thus, my now-kindergartener has several compilation tapes and CDs to his name. He has one entirely devoted to Andrew Lloyd Webber musicals, another filled with PBS "Kideo" favorites, one of Big Band hits (thanks to my husband), one with various Disney tunes and, yes, even a tape of toe-tapping pop/rock/country gems that span several decades of radio.

Of course, our son long ago outgrew the confines of the stroller. He's a big kid now who can go anywhere I can go, do anything I can do. Maybe even better.

"I wanna walk *next* to you, Mommy," he informed me recently, motioning to the door with his music in one hand while holding his other palm open and out to me, waiting for me to grasp it. "I wanna hold your hand."

As I wondered if, perhaps, the time was right to introduce my son to the Beatles, I grabbed his chubby fingers and agreed immediately to his request. Now, sometimes, we walk together—to the beat of different drummers, it's true—but we're side-by-side, hand-in-hand. And you can't beat that.

INSOMNIA

The spirit of the
firefly flitters on in
my night-light, sleepless.

ON MOTHERS, DAUGHTERS, SONS, AND WORRYING

I am both a mother and a daughter. But I'm not the mother *of* a daughter, a fact that I have spent considerable time pondering.

When we first learned from the nice ultrasound lady that our child would be a son, I was secretly relieved. I did not express this relief to my friends or family, however, because then I would've had to explain that my fears of pregnancy went beyond the typical "Is It A Healthy Baby?" worry. Once we were assured of the blessing of good health, though, my anxiety of actual parenthood took hold, and I realized I was going to be in way over my head no matter what the circumstance or which gender the child turned out to be. But I'd *really* be in trouble with a daughter.

Why?

Well, for starters, because I'd fallen prey to the common misconception that mothers had more to worry about with their daughters, and because I knew firsthand that issues between a mom and her little girl could arise out of nowhere…from those intrinsic mother-daughter comparisons to the identity issues that can linger for decades to the natural woman-to-woman semblances that come with femininity...take your pick.

By contrast, I figured I could handle a son with much less anxiety because he was, by genetic design, my opposite. No one expects a son to base his character, his profession, or his appearance on his mother the way that same expectation hovers over a daughter. No one says cutesy things to a boy like "Are you going to grow up to be like your mommy someday?" No one will ever retort, "Oh, you sound just like your mother on the phone. I couldn't tell your voices apart!" No one will scrutinize his appearance after studying mine and comment on how alike we look in any way except, perhaps, to note that we have similar eyes or share a few facial features.

My dear child would be safe from all those admittedly stereotypic female foibles I wouldn't want to pass onto the next generation, such as my various food neuroses that always seemed to start with "But I LOVE chocolate" and end with "Um, do my thighs look horribly fat now?" He would likewise be free from those areas where I've let my more feminine sisters down, i.e., my inability to make a sheet cake from scratch or my supreme lack of fashion sense, which, in certain circles, is seen as a significant deficiency indeed. (Just my attachment to baggy sweatshirts and yoga pants alone is a stylistic problem that might well embarrass a more in vogue daughter amidst her peers.)

Then there's my stunning ignorance of shoe shopping. I know, I know. I shouldn't confess this publicly, but I don't really like shopping of any kind. And I don't *know* shoes or designers or anything at all about cool accessories. For years I was convinced that Jimmy Choo's was some kind of great

Chinese take-out place in New York.

Oh, and furthermore, I wasn't drawn as a kid to super-girly activities like cheerleading, ballet, or even gymnastics (beyond a very short Nadia Comaneci phase in 1976). Nothing at all wrong with these athletic endeavors, but they just weren't for me.

Of course, I was certain that if I had a daughter, she would be exactly the type of child to adore every single one of the pursuits in which I either had no interest or no proficiency. She'd find me a tremendous disappointment, and the hurt would stay with me forever.

So I was grateful for a baby boy. I figured that most of the upcoming parent-child comparisons would fall directly into my husband's camp, which eased my own parental panic considerably. See? I wouldn't have to worry about raising a son nearly as much.

As it turned out, my logic was a bit faulty.

Guess which sport my son finds most intriguing? That's right. Gymnastics. Guess who's a bigger chocoholic than me? Yep. Same kid. And while he and his daddy do share many rough-and-tumble activities together, my little boy is also very fond of baking and shopping. (Although, thankfully, he couldn't care less about shoes.)

The numerous qualms I'd imagined experiencing as the mother of a daughter are so often the very same fears I have now for my son. I fret over his acceptance by his peers and his ability to make true friends. I stress over his eating habits, body image, health. I note the similarities between us—which, incidentally, ended up being a lot more profound than eye color—and I have minor anxiety attacks over things like his sensitivity to pessimism or his safety in a crowd or his burgeoning awareness of existential issues. Being such a

Wanderlust in Suburbia

Class-A Worrier myself, I even worry about him worrying.

Many moms I've talked to over the years expressed the same thing: They worry about their children equally and powerfully, regardless of the child's gender. At times, the anxieties for one child might overshadow their anxieties for another, but the intensity of their worry balances out, whether it's for a son or a daughter. And all of them fear leaving any kind of negative imprint on their children's psyches.

I'm reminded of my own mom who, though very different in temperament and areas of personal interest from my brother and me, always encouraged us in the activities we loved. Even when our choices seemed to completely mystify her. Or when she worried about us, which was almost all of the time. Or when we changed our minds and she had to regroup and learn all about our latest passions.

My brother and I are both in our thirties, with jobs and homes of our own now and, yet, she still calls frequently to check up on us…to make sure we're healthy and happy. I'm starting to realize that this brand of motherhood fretfulness not only never goes away, it never even wavers.

So, Happy Mother's Day…to all the mothers of daughters and all the mothers of sons. I've come to believe that a mother's influence strongly marks her children, even when she doesn't plan on it. And that a mother's love expands to encompass pastimes she never would've considered on her own, simply because of a wish to support her children. And that a mother wants to be assured of her children's well being, no matter where they are in life or what they're doing.

So, if you can, call yours up and tell her about what's been happening in your world. Chances are, she's *very* interested.

She cares deeply. And she's worried about you. Because, whether you're her son or daughter, that's what mothers do.

REMEMBERING UNSTRUCTURED TIME

Summer... The word reminds me of long, hot afternoons in the Midwest. Mosquitoes attacking us on the back patio. My rickety, metal swing set as a kid. The ice cream truck. And that catchy '80s song "Magic" by The Cars.

To my son—with the notable exception of the ice cream truck—summertime runs at an altogether different speed. To him it means summer-school enrichment classes or day camp activities. Sporting events to rush off to. Organized playdates and planned get-togethers at the pool. Although there are still plenty of mosquitoes buzzing around, our family doesn't tend to lounge on the back patio the way my parents, my brother, and I did a few decades ago. We always seem to have somewhere to go.

And, though our summer calendar may differ greatly from our school-year schedule, I've come to realize our lives aren't significantly less busy during June, July, and August. It's a different kind of chaos, certainly, but it's chaos nonetheless.

The sentimental side of me revels in memories of my elementary school summers, recollecting endless stretches of unstructured time, and I miss the possibility of creating a similar experience for my own child. To be honest, I think the concept of "just playing outside all day" would be as foreign to him as a culture-language immersion program in Bratislava. I find myself wondering what happened in the world during the intervening years to make his expectations for our warm-weather months so unlike what my own had been, and I try to imagine ways to get back some of the open-ended summertime magic that I loved so much. For all our sakes.

Of course, when I compare and contrast my son's generation to mine, I realize the differences are profound. Some of you may remember the 1970s. (It's okay. You don't have to admit it.) You'll recall, we didn't have iPods then. Sure, we had *disco*...but most people wouldn't consider that much of a consolation. We also didn't have home computers, hi-tech videogames, or the Internet. Furthermore, cell phones, answering machines, microwaves, and VCRs/DVDs/TiVo/DVRs were all the stuff of sci-fi novels. And, incidentally, so were the expectations that went along with such advanced technology.

Ultimately, I think that's what it comes down to: Rising societal expectations that have trickled down to the elementary-age set.

Today, with technology making global communication easier, faster and more accessible, we're all expected to be "reachable" whenever someone wants to contact us. Back in my childhood, if we were on a family walk or out to dinner or visiting someone and one of my friends tried to call me at home, I missed the call. And guess what the friend did? If she really wanted to talk to me, she called back later.

Now, if someone wants to get ahold of us, they have our home number, our cell number, our work numbers, our voice mail and, if all else fails, a variety of email addresses. It's seen as wildly inconsiderate, not only to fail to immediately respond to a message, but to even make someone leave a message. ("You went out *without* your cell phone? But, *why?*") Living dangerously, I guess.

We're also seen as living on the edge if we fail to grab every educational advantage for our kids. Children from preschool-age onward are now expected to have remedial assistance in any area of perceived mediocrity, formal lessons in all subjects that might get them "ahead in life," and enrichment classes in everything else.

When I was growing up, if public schools offered summer classes, it was primarily for kids who needed serious help with skill reinforcement. Sure, there were some enrichment activities available, but they were usually expensive, seven days at most, and it was rare any of my friends or I went away to such things for longer than that. Even my super-athletic brother didn't do more than a weeklong sleep-away sports camp. The rest of his summer he spent hanging out—in the driveway, for the most part—playing basketball with his neighborhood buddies and, periodically, going on a fun-run.

Then there's travel. Kids now are expected to be well accustomed to airport security. To have a global worldview. To rack up their own frequent flyer miles, even. To be a "cultured kid" these days means exposure to resort-level golf, high-end art museums, and the occasional London musical. For those of us fortunate to live near a major metropolis like Chicago, culture often comes to us. Everyone else is expected to hunt it down or vacation near it.

As a kid, we didn't go on many long car trips—gas prices were horrendous back then (which, I guess, means some things haven't changed at all). There were no DVD players in my parents' minivan or SUV. Also: There weren't minivans and SUVs. My mom and dad drove a 4-door sedan that my brother and I would cram our stuff and ourselves into—although, a few of our friends did have spacious station wagons.

The landscape of our highways, our subdivisions and our world *has* changed in the past thirty years, and it presents us, at times, with some very real dangers.

I was at the park recently and overheard a conversation between two women. They were discussing their summer plans and the signing up of their children for various classes because, as one beleaguered mom explained to the other, "I can't have them around the house all day."

Now, I doubt this mother was saying this because she didn't want to spend time with her kids. But, whether the world is really less safe today or we're simply more aware of the perils, children don't play outside for as long anymore, and rarely without adults nearby. Parents tend to be busier career-wise—working more hours out of financial necessity (either at outside locations or at home offices) and, thus, not available to supervise their children for as long. The classes, day camps, etc. serve as a safe place for kids to spend their summers.

And, so, with the way our world is structured today, it goes against the grain to "just do nothing" for three months. I hear people all the time saying they're striving for simplicity. I've tried to do it, too. Right now, though, I'm merely striving for better a sense of priority. I don't know if it's possible to return to a simpler style of life, or if the current ways and means of society make it impossible to reverse the tide of over-expectation, but I can try to at least limit the chaos by focusing on the handful of activities that matter most to my family and me.

Here's hoping somehow, somewhere in this summer that we'll all be able to find a few unstructured hours for lounging on that back patio. Hold the mosquitoes.

WANDERLUST IN SUBURBIA

I have a confession: Beneath my fruit-snack-toting, suburban mother façade hides the soul of a travel junky. As I drive my seven-year-old son to birthday parties, taking the sluggish I-94, I imagine whizzing toward exotic European locations via the Autobahn instead.

After my good friend recounts her walking tour through northern Scotland, I envision myself trailing in her footsteps, battling the fog, the mist and the shadow of Nessy as I trudge through rain-soaked, northern Illinois soccer fields.

When my young, single brother—who, like Jane Austen's Mr. Darcy, is in possession of a good fortune—plans his two-week vacation to Hawaii, I vicariously feel the sun warming my face on a stroll along the historic Dole Plantation grounds. I need only to plunge my fork into a bowl of tangy pineapple chunks to inspire the illusion.

For a few moments every day I engage in a version of Walter-Middy Mom. I forget all about play dates, classroom volunteering, cell-phone calls, and the unholy mountain of laundry in the hamper. I'm a traveler, and I'm *going* somewhere.

Somewhere besides the grocery store.

"Why are we buying THAT, Mommy?" my little boy asks, tones of horror lacing his voice.

We're in the middle of the store's Aisle 5, and I'm reverently holding up a jar of artichoke hearts, reminiscing about a delicious salad a Sicilian friend once made for me. The recipe calls for marinated artichokes, black olives, diced tomatoes, brightly colored peppers, and rotini pasta, among other ingredients. Although I've never visited Palermo, I can almost feel the pulse of Sicily's capital city and smell the enticing aroma of oregano and olive oil.

"Mommy, I want macaroni and cheese. You promised we could get some. And SpaghettiOs."

Well, okay. This is the accepted pasta of my son's generation, although somewhat less authentically Italian than what I had in mind. Before we shuffle to the checkout line, we work out a compromise and agree on fresh (not canned) ravioli, but the gourmet chef in my imagination insists upon a bolder dinner next time. I try. Yet, some of my more ambitious attempts at foreign cuisine are met with grimaces that could turn a mythic goddess to stone.

"No chicken drumsticks or stuffing tonight?" my husband asks, inspecting my homemade attempt at Thai vegetarian spring rolls on his dinner plate. He stabs an extra-firm square of tofu with his knife and wrinkles his nose thoughtfully. "Kind of squishy, this stuff."

All in all, sometimes Chef Boyardee is the way to go.

I love my husband, my son and our family life—make no mistake. Because I love them, I willingly defrost chicken and try to come up with acceptable, yet healthful, ways to fix it. I watch PBS Kids, viewing episodes of *Arthur* and *George Shrinks* I've long since memorized. And I spend my free time hunting for library books on the terrible T-Rex or the equally intriguing SpongeBob. Although I tackle these chores joyfully most days, this still does not keep me from daydreaming about faraway places and decidedly non-suburban adventures.

It is, perhaps, the prerogative of families to form a unit onto themselves. To merge and become "one" from the collective of individuals who share a life together. Every member sacrifices a little bit of his or her freedom in order to keep home routines running smoothly. The tendency, though, is for such a cohesive family to forget that the people who comprise the unit—especially for those of us taking on the roles of "Mommy" or "Daddy"—are people who once lived very different lives and played very different roles.

When I was in college, I belonged to a dance troupe that toured Europe for six weeks. We performed all styles of American dance at folk festivals in four countries. We met fascinating musicians and dancers from around the globe. We feasted nightly on "specialties of the region." And, when we returned home, I swore that dancing, traveling, and exotic dining would remain part of my lifelong personal identity.

Uh, huh.

Nearly twenty years later, my dancing repertoire primarily consists of wiggling and jiggling to tunes from a Disney soundtrack. The last time I tangoed was in 1993. Travel-wise, my husband and I consider a visit to my native Wisconsin a "Big Adventure" these days. And I can't tell you the last time I ordered anything from a menu that a first grader wouldn't recognize.

But call off the detectives. There are no hidden mysteries here. In the dozen years since our wedding, we went from two singles to a married couple with a child. From two full-time incomes to only one. From a one-bedroom loft apartment to a three-bedroom house. And let's not even talk about taxes, inflation, and the skyrocketing cost of education. We used to have time, money, and energy to pursue our individual interests with ease. Then times changed.

And they're likely to change again.

As our son grows and breaks away from our family unit to forge his own identity, his father and I must be there to support and encourage him. Just as we lovingly camouflaged some of our own individuality during his early childhood in order to create this strong familial unity, we must be willing to let him break apart from it so he can thrive and evolve into his own man. A man who seeks the tasks and hobbies that stir his soul. Voyages to distant places in search of the people and locations that resonate within him. And tries new dishes to determine his own taste and style.

It is then, perhaps, that my son might welcome my culinary adventurousness. When my dancing time might be reclaimed. When my husband can enjoy more frequently some of his long-lost pastimes also—his chess games, tennis matches, biking. When we two parents can plan that dreamed-of cruise to the Caribbean…with the expectation of actually going on it.

Maybe.

Once braces, soccer uniforms, driver's education fees, and college tuition are paid. Once our monthly bills don't have us seeing hazy green spots when we close our eyes. Once we feel assured that we really did put our child first and he is happily settled into a life of his own choosing.

Until that time I must be content with my Walter-Middy Mom world. I read and often review novels that allow me to escape to Paris or Sydney or Rio de Janeiro, and I imagine myself in a more glamorous, fruit-snack-free environment. I rent movies where the heroes and heroines lounge in Tuscany, sipping red wine on a veranda, never going faster than a motor-scooter spin through the hilly countryside. A place where they probably eat meals with marinated artichoke hearts daily, and everyone loves it.

    I'm reminded, too, of that Nitty Gritty Dirt Band song "An American Dream," the one where we're supposed to "think Jamaican in the moonlight…" I've never been to Jamaica. But someday soon, I know, when I'm sprinkling shredded coconut on someone's birthday cake, I'll imagine what it might like. Sandy beaches. Rum. Love every night. And getting there by just closing my eyes.

JOURNALS AS TIME MACHINES OF MOTHERHOOD

Lately I've been thinking about journaling—the simple task of jotting down the smattering of thoughts that skitter through my mind on any given day—an activity that's been part of my life for 25 years.

One of the things I've always liked about it is that it requires me to pause and mark in indelible ink what I'm preoccupied with at specific moments in time. Much of this is admittedly mundane drivel, the reading of which could drive a sane soul to homicide, but it's my life and I must embrace the foolishness alongside the more sublime moments.

Still, I laugh aloud when I flip through my powder-blue adolescent journal with the "safety lock" to protect its many secrets. Hard to believe anyone, at any point in time, would've been mesmerized by my fourteen-year-old self declaring, "Oh! Steve smiled at me in study hall today!" Really riveting stuff, let me tell you, and a bit worrisome in that I'm always left wondering if, perhaps, I missed out on telling the "important" details amidst all the pages of nonsense.

From the perspective of more than two decades,

however, I've discovered that a few of those old journal notes gain power with the passing years. Some even shed surprising insight on a state of mind I could not appreciate fully at the time.

Case in point: I recently reread the entries from my first six months of motherhood. During that fuzzy, surrealistic period of being overwhelmed by the enormity of the task I'd just accepted, I remember surprisingly little without assistance. What I recall with clarity was my zombie-like state of sleep deprivation, my perpetual sense of new-mother panic over the 7,453 baby-care maneuvers I might fail to do correctly, the awe-inspiring surge of adoration I felt for my newborn, and my conviction that I was now tied to the future of humanity through the miracle of parenthood.

The rest of my life during this period remains a mystery. Unearthing old journals, however, gives me the ability to relive and, consequently, re-*see* bits of those days with the wisdom I've ostensibly gained in the intervening years.

One evening when my son was just over two months old, I wrote: *"Beautiful smiles and ferocious screams...our son is certainly a baby of contrasts."* At the time, I was referring to his changeable behavior on one specific day, but the gift of years has proven that my experience was more universal. In many ways, all children are a study in extremes, and they can contradict themselves daily. This is a necessity of growth, for they must figure out what they DON'T like and what they DON'T want in this life as much as they need to discover what they DO. Somewhere along life's journey, we become adults capable of moderation, and the outbursts of fierce displeasure, appearing rapidly on the heels of intense elation, become tempered.

But back then I couldn't reason away my newborn's behavior. I wondered only, *What did I do to upset this kid? What will make him gurgle with happiness again? What dearth of logic made me think becoming a mother was a good idea?* It's reassuring to be able to go back and find the source of some of those worries and look at those early days of parenthood with a clearer eye.

Last summer I took part in a journaling project in which about 500 American women, on an uneventful Tuesday in late June, wrote down what transpired in our "day" (the same 24-hour period for all of us). Women across the country expressed their fears of war or unpaid bills or family illness. In some cases we had major issues to deal with that day. In others, it was merely the little things in life we needed to tackle.

The observations I jotted down for my "Day Diary" were full of the tedium of stay-at-home motherhood, or so I thought at the time. I recently reread a section of it, though—a part where I'd written about how our son paddled into our bedroom to awaken my husband and me, much as he always does. My words were throwaway comments, transitional sentences explaining how the first phase of my day began. But today, over a year later, the beauty of the commonplace behavior I'd recorded struck a deeper note in me.

As much as our darling son has honed his extremes of temperament (to only an occasional tantrum, thank goodness), he has also remained strikingly consistent in some areas. He still tiptoes into our bedroom every morning—just as he did as a toddler, just as he did last June—and wedges his way in between us. He still likes to snuggle under our covers, squirm until the sheets are twisted like a mini funnel cloud, and rouse us by his earnest attempt at being quiet.

After a few minutes of this, when sleep has become too impossible a task, I usually flip over and study his face. His body is bigger now, of course, and his personality more powerful than the baby he'd once been, but I'm always amazed at how his features have held fast throughout the years. When his dark eyelashes lay against his rounded cheeks and he's curled into a slumbering ball next to me, the past intermingles with the present. It's as though his six years of childhood melts into the air, my newborn is with me again, and I'm a young mother once more.

And later, when I read another old journal entry that mentions in passing some tiny detail of our child's behavior, some seemingly inconsequential thing he said, I remember this moment of watching him sleep…preceded by *years* of watching him…and I realize I'd sent a message through time to my son's future mom in those journals.

That nothing is as insignificant as it seems.

That I'd inadvertently written down the most important stuff after all.

EXCERPT FROM
THE ROAD AND BEYOND

Relating to some of my favorite subjects—motherhood, journals, travel, music, and family secrets—is my most recently released novel, *The Road and Beyond*. It's a romantic women's fiction mystery that features a road trip down Historic Route 66 (the "Mother Road") and it involves two parallel storylines, which take place decades apart. Here's a little more about the book, followed by an excerpt:

The Road and Beyond is the expanded book-club edition of *The Road to You*. It contains not only the completed original story set in the late 1970s, but it also includes the brand-new present-day tale of Aurora, now a mature and married woman with two adult sons, who must confront her worst parental nightmare.

One Disappearance Had Been Enough To Last Her A Lifetime...

Aurora Gray is no stranger to tragedy. In the summer of 1976, when she was just sixteen, her world turned upside down when her big brother Gideon and his best friend Jeremy disappeared. For two years, there's no word from either of them. No trace of their whereabouts. But then, shortly after her high-school graduation, she unexpectedly finds her brother's journal and sees that it's been written in again. Recently. By him.

There are secret messages coded within the journal's pages and Aurora, who is unusually perceptive and a natural puzzle solver, is determined to follow where they lead, no matter what the cost. She confides in the only person she feels might help her interpret the clues: Donovan McCafferty, Jeremy's older brother and a guy she's always been drawn to...even against her better judgment.

The two of them set out on a road trip of discovery and danger, heading westward along America's historic Route 66 in search of their siblings and the answers to questions they haven't dared to ask aloud. The mystery they uncover will forever change the course of their lives.

...But Now It Was Happening Again

Decades later, in the summer of 2014, fifty-four-year-old Aurora receives a terrifying phone call—her adult son Charlie is missing—and this news inevitably brings the memories of her adolescent years rushing back. Haunting recollections she'd hoped to keep buried.

Were the choices she'd made in her youth responsible for her son's disappearance now? And how on earth can she find him—quickly—so that she might be able to prevent the trauma of the past from repeating itself?

The novel is currently available in paperback and ebook, and it will soon be released in audio as well. Hope you'll enjoy this sample of the story!

An Excerpt from THE ROAD AND BEYOND (2014)

"All journeys have secret destinations of which the traveler is unaware."
~Martin Buber

~*~

"Hindsight is 20/20."
~Unknown

AURORA'S NOTES
Pasadena, California ~ Summer 2020

It's been forty-two years since the summer of 1978. The summer I was seventeen going on eighteen. The summer I found Gideon's journal.

We didn't have then what's so commonplace now: cell phones, wireless Internet and all of our twenty-first century devices. No routine DNA testing, GPS or forensic anthropology experts like the ones so prevalent today, even on nighttime TV. If we'd had these then, it might have all been different, of course. I might have gotten my questions answered sooner, more easily.

Or maybe not. Knowing what happened six years ago, maybe it would have been just as mystifying, only more hi-tech.

Some things I do know from my vantage point in the future, however, and I guess if there's a year to look back on the past with perfect clarity, 2020 would be that year.

I would have likely felt less disconnected from my peers if I'd realized when I was younger that there were others like me out there. Those who didn't possess any kind of extrasensory power, per se, but for whom the world was a tapestry of intuitive impulses and observations. People who were simply more perceptive than most. More aware of everything.

But teens are notoriously self-involved. They can't help but think they're "special"—a quality they simultaneously crave and dread. This colored my perceptions back then, I know.

One day, perhaps, I'll chronicle the years between the memorable summer that defined the end of my adolescence and the weekend six summers ago that forever marked my adulthood. Especially as a mother.

But not now.

Now I need to share a memory. Or two, I guess. Reminiscences that unite the past with the present. The earliest ones are Kodacolor snapshots of a time that is no longer—complete with weighty, cumbersome reflections I'd worked hard to shed in my twenties, thirties, even forties, as if they were layers of warm clothing I could strip off in relief when summer began.

Only, the seasons are cyclical, and summer is a fleeting little sparrow.

Which is why, after these long decades, I've found it's best to be truthful about the past, not try to bury it in my waking unconscious. Age has a tendency to sharpen our internal vision. At sixty years old, I crave lucidity, precision, freedom from constraint. I may have gained the ability to dance around in the heavy fabric of ambiguity, but I've lost all desire to do it.

So, in answer to a question I was once asked at seventeen, I'll say boldly that, yes, I know exactly where my moral compass can be found, and I can read it clearly. I know who my traveling companions are, too—those who've been truest to me over time.

As proof, I present my assembly of carefully reconstructed recollections of youth and family...of history and journeys...of loss and

love. And of finding oneself again by retracing a handful of unforgettable steps.
~Aurora, 7-1-20

~*~

"There are only two mistakes one can make along the road to the truth; not going all the way, and not starting."
~Buddha

CHAPTER ONE
Chameleon Lake, Minnesota ~ Thursday, June 8, 1978

My hands trembled as I unlocked the cedar box in the tool shed. I listened for the distinctive click, lifted the lid and peered inside, not knowing what I'd find in its shadowy depths.

I half expected to see my old diary resting at the bottom, even though I knew it was safely back in my room. I used to hide it in here years ago, before the key to the box was lost. A key that mysteriously resurfaced this week.

But it wasn't my diary.

Instead, I found a different book. The small brown-leather journal that had once belonged to my older brother, Gideon. My only sibling. The one who'd disappeared two years ago. The one everyone said was dead.

I bit back the usual sob that always rose up in my throat when I remembered him, then stared at the medium-sized box and its contents, almost afraid to touch anything. To my eye, my brother's book seemed to have been conjured there, as if by magic. I hadn't seen Gideon's journal since the day he'd gone missing... What was written in it? And why, all of a sudden, had it reappeared—much like the key to this box—here, now?

Before I could talk myself out of it, I snatched up the journal and began to examine it.

Funny, even with the impression of a delicate butterfly stamped on the front cover, the book still managed to be tinged with Gideon's masculinity. To an outsider, it probably looked like it contained some kid's observations on nature. Something safe, simple, innocuous.

And the first few pages really were ordinary. So typical of my big brother that I caught myself in a sigh, missing him. I still missed him so damned much—with every breath, every memory.

Like the way he'd grin at me whenever I saw him scribbling in it. Even if I teased him about the butterfly or keeping secrets or writing notes about his girlfriends, he'd just laugh.

"Aurora, I love butterflies and secrets...*and* girls," he'd tell me, amused and so self-confident.

But here I was, skimming through a dozen pages, and I hadn't found any dating exploits yet. Just details about cars and engines cluttering the first third of the journal. I spotted a step-by-step flowchart for performing an oil change. Something about the testing of transmission fluid. A procedure for fixing a leaky head gasket and the supplies needed to do so:

1 gallon antifreeze
1 radiator drainage pan
1 quart engine block sealer

...and so on.

Wanderlust in Suburbia

Looked kind of like a recipe to me.

Lists of standard adjustable wrenches (*8"/203mm, 10"/254mm, 12"/305mm*) and screwdrivers (*Torx #15, Phillips #00*) followed. I squinted at them all. For a girly, bookish seventeen-year-old like me, this was about as riveting as reading an old J.C. Penney catalog.

I kept reading anyway, my heart pounding as I traced my brother's words with my fingertip. The familiar raw ache twisted deeper.

On the page, Gideon was going on for an eternity and a half, specifying the differences between long nose pliers and nippers but, truth was, I didn't care. I knew the only reason I continued to flip the jaundiced, grease-stained pages was because this journal had once belonged to *him*. Just seeing that curious cramped script of his—far less even and so much smaller than my own—made me feel as though he were standing next to me, instructing me on something yet again. And Gideon had liked to teach lessons…when he was alive.

I shoved back at least fifty memories of my warm, funny, clever big brother, grasping for the emotional anesthesia that I knew cool over-analysis would bring—my default setting ever since he'd been gone. The same questions kept running through my head, but I didn't have any answers.

Why was this journal here? Why was I finding it now?

But then I turned the page once more and read a line that made me stop short.

The strangeness of what I saw left me struggling to inhale the musty air of the tool shed, and I felt tiny shivers sweep like lightning crackles across my skin.

The date somewhere in the middle of the page was from April 1976, but notated in the upper right-hand corner was a much more recent date: *Monday, May 29, 1978.*

Memorial Day. Less than two weeks ago.

I checked and double-checked the numbers, almost positive my eyesight was playing tricks on me in the dim light. I had to be misreading this. It *couldn't* be real.

A few months after Gideon disappeared, the cops told us he must be dead. Insisted it had to be true. And due to the force of *everyone's* conviction, my parents and I had been persuaded to accept the police's assessment...although, I could never quite squelch the flicker of hope that lurked in my heart and flared up at the oddest moments. I could never really stop believing that *everyone* might just be wrong.

And now I had this.

Underneath the recent date were the words: *Start here. G.*

Logical or not, it was as if this were a message written just for me. Oh, God. Could it be?

My brain swam in a soup of questions and possibilities, a mix of elements and matter. Whos, hows and whens. Origins and endings. My hidden flicker of hope burst into flame.

There had been a lot of strangers filtering through our town over Memorial Day weekend—visitors from places nearby, friends and relatives of residents, the occasional herd of curious wildlife—for the annual Chameleon Fest. Three days of hastily assembled carnival rides, taste tests, fireworks in the evening. A weekend of some small excitement in our otherwise sleepy lakeside village.

And then the key to the cedar box reappeared.

It had been lost for ages but, out of nowhere, it materialized again. In my room. In my desk. In my plastic paperclip tray.

Gideon used to tease me about how much I loved personalized stationery and office supplies. All of my neatly stacked notepads. My smooth-writing Bic pens. My colored bulletin-board tacks. For a couple of days, I tried to dismiss my discovery. I tried to convince myself I'd just overlooked the key in my numbness of the past two years.

But the jab of peculiarity pressed upon my senses and only grew stronger.

It was *too* strange to have found the key there, buried beneath a sea of paperclips, since I knew I'd replenished them just a few weeks ago. Even in grief, I wasn't someone who'd forget something like that. And I couldn't keep denying my instincts.

Standing here in the middle of the tool shed and holding Gideon's journal, I knew for sure that finding this key couldn't have been accidental. Like the trajectory of a pinball, if you hit the metal flapper so it connected with the ball in just the right, sweet spot, it would send the orb rolling with a smack, straight into the diamond center and—*bing, bing, bing, bing, bing*—you'd get the 10,000-point bonus.

The person who put the key in my paperclip bin *knew* I'd eventually find it, recognize it and head to the tool shed to hunt down the cedar box.

The person who put the key in my paperclip bin *knew* how organized I was, how much of a puzzle solver I'd always been and that I wouldn't stop looking until I'd found the box, opened it and discovered the journal resting there.

And the *only* someone who would know these things about me was my brother.

Somehow, Gideon must have come into town on Memorial Day weekend, snuck into the house while we were away and left the key for me, knowing the path he'd set me on.

Bing, bing, bing, bing, bing.

I felt myself slam into the 10,000-point bonus, my mind

reeling. I tried to shake the mental machine hard enough to clear my head. *Flash. Bing. Tilt.*

But it was too late. My world had already tilted and, suddenly, I knew I was playing a very different game.

~*~

I wandered back to our house, my brain still swirling and Gideon's voice—loud and insistent—in my mind.

"You *can't* tell," I could almost hear him say. A line from our childhood that he'd used more than once when he was doing something dangerous.

"Mom and Dad will freak," he'd add. Then he'd laugh and try to reassure me.

"Oh, stop worrying, Sis. They don't have to know everything all the time."

"We're not kids anymore. We can handle this."

"Trust me, it'll be fine. Really."

And it usually was…until it wasn't. Until, one day, he was gone.

Any normal person would've ignored the pleading voice from the past and run, not walked, to the telephone, to call her still-grieving parents. To give them a surge of hope that their missing son might be alive after all. Because, oh, God—I didn't want to witness even another minute of my parents' pain. Not if it was within my power to stop it.

But I wasn't a totally normal person. I knew intuitively—with a mysterious certainty I'd come to expect and rely on—that this wasn't what Gideon wanted. He didn't want my parents to find the journal. He wanted *me* to find it.

Me alone.

Otherwise, he would have left it in the middle of the

dining room table, the place he'd always tossed his school notes when we were little kids, his car keys as we got older, his wallet and, sometimes, an empty beer can or Twinkie wrapper. It was *his* spot. Mine was the edge of the kitchen counter, just beneath Granny's Bavarian cuckoo clock. Nonverbal signals that we were home.

So, I didn't tell Mom or Dad.

Instead, I took the journal to my room—a deceptively cheery place I hadn't bothered to alter since Gideon's disappearance. It still held the relics of my life from two years ago. All of my interests frozen at fifteen.

My poster of David Cassidy was the cheeriest item of all, although I'd finally gotten over my crush on him. I now preferred men who weren't teen heartthrobs. Who were older, cooler and more serious. Like Harrison Ford.

I flopped onto my tie-dyed bedspread, took a half-dozen deep breaths and flipped further through the journal. It was all written in Gideon's distinctive scrawl. Really, no forger could ever replicate those peculiar loops and lines.

"It's like a fifth grader's writing," I'd told him mockingly once. I, Aurora Gray, the superior younger sister in matters of penmanship.

He flicked his eyes toward the ceiling. "Maybe I don't want just *anyone* to be able to read it," he retorted. "Maybe content is more important than style. Ever consider that, Miss Straight-A Student?" Then he winked at me and went back to whatever he was doing. Good-natured as always, though secretive. Delighting too much in his cageyness.

I read through every single page in the book, but my brother's notes didn't make much sense to me. Cities, sometimes states, with a handful of names listed, usually an equation or two. More car parts, chemical fluids, a smattering of tools. It was like a crash course in auto mechanics with an extra-credit seminar in geography—all in code.

Thanks a lot, Gideon. How useful.

My pulse raced at what this all might mean, though. And, again, my brother's corner note kept me looking, studying, scrutinizing.

"Start here."

Start here...what? Start reading? Start traveling to these places? Start piecing together a way to find him? If so, why would he have made this so hard for me? Sure, we used to play at codes a lot as kids, but did he really think games would be necessary now?

I heard a set of heavy footsteps in the far hall, shuffling in a way that signaled a thump of recognition low on my spine. Dad was home. A so-so work day at the post office. I exhaled in relief. There were never *good* days any more. Gloomy was normal, and tolerable was the new excellent. How long had it been since we'd stopped expecting anything above barely okay?

Long.

"Hello, Aurora," he called to me, his voice tired, slightly hoarse.

"Hi, Dad," I called back and then waited, on high alert, until my father had walked past my room without coming in. Mom wasn't expected home for another half hour from her secretarial job, so I had a little more time. I intended to use it.

I scanned another page of Gideon's journal—just as cryptic as the rest, but this time I noticed a reference to "J." This, too, sent my mind rolling in a prescribed direction.

The "J," I knew, stood for "Jeremy," as in the younger of the two McCafferty brothers. He and Gideon were best friends, and they would both be twenty years old right now if they were, in fact, wandering any part of the planet jointly or separately. They'd disappeared together on that same day.

My heartbeat picked up the pace as I flipped back to the *Start here* page and reread it, more carefully this time. Slipped in between the gauges and chemical substances I couldn't identify was the date: *Monday, April 19, 1976*. Just a few months before they'd gone missing. And this was followed by the words: *J. & I drove to Crescent Cove.*

Where the hell was Crescent Cove?

I whipped out the dog-eared U.S. atlas from under my bed, brushing the threads of a spider's web off the cover and coughing as the dust particles swirled around me. Then I studied the state map of Minnesota. Looked in the city index, too, but I couldn't find any place with that name. There was a La Crescent, a Crescent Beach, a Crescent Bay...

But, as I was about to toss the book away, I saw it at the edge of the page. It was there in nearly microscopic print, just across the Wisconsin border, near the Saint Croix Chippewa Indian Reservation. About three and a half hours away. If I got in my car and started driving eastward, I'd get there by nine tonight.

And then...do what?

I turned back to the journal, inspecting it for hints. Clues. Anything to tell me the correct next step.

I had no trouble catching vibes off people, and I'd read Gideon's expressions well enough when he was here. His journal, however, couldn't gesture frantically or blink in surprise. It couldn't tell me any of the three thousand things other people said with their fidgety fingers, raised eyebrows and bitten bottom lips. It was just a collection of words on old paper.

But it was a collection of words that was branded in ink,

probably by my brother, as recently as ten days ago. And if it was proof that Gideon was still alive—and if my instincts about him having left our town for a reason had been right all along—then Jeremy might be alive, too. Was that possible?

I could almost feel the pinball of connectivity rolling between the different centers of knowledge and recognition in my brain, leading inevitably to the *one other person* who not only had an immediate, strong and highly personal stake in the outcome of this question, but who also had a solid mechanical background. Somebody who might be able to draw secret understandings from words that, to me, resembled a form of hieroglyphic gibberish.

That would be Jeremy's older brother, Donovan.

Oh, crap.

~*~

I could count on one hand the things I knew were true about Donovan McCafferty:

He was twenty-three—just over five years older than I was.

He'd escaped into the army at age eighteen and, except for a few quick but memorable visits, hadn't returned to Minnesota until this past winter.

He had an excellent mechanical mind.

And he made me very nervous.

Underneath my skin, every nerve fiber was fast twitching. Just thinking about Donovan always did that to me but, this time, it was also about the trip.

I couldn't have been more impatient to get on the road to Crescent Cove, and I really didn't want to make a stop at Donovan's workplace. But, awkward though it would be, he knew a few things I didn't. And he just might signal to me (whether he realized it or not) some very useful directions.

I waited until after dinner, biding my time. Made the three of us broiled chicken, mashed potatoes, broccoli. Boring, yes, but it wasn't like anyone cared.

Then I excused myself from the usual watching of TV news and Thursday-night shows—they were repeat episodes anyway—and drove to the only auto-repair shop and gas station in town. The one I avoided like the plague whenever possible, preferring to fill up in places where no one knew me, like Alexandria or St. Cloud. Places where Donovan McCafferty...wasn't.

It was 7:05 p.m. by the time I got to the shop, and I parked a fair distance from the entrance. They closed at seven, but the work light in the back was on and two out of the three garage doors were still open. I knew he was in there. Not because I'd caught even one glimpse of Mr. Tall, Dark and Intense yet, but because the only other car in the lot was a crimson Trans Am with the giant Firebird decal in black and gold across the hood. His, of course.

I pushed open my car door, grabbed my tote bag with Gideon's journal tucked safely inside and inhaled several lungfuls of the cloying summer air. So early in June and already every breath was wrapped in sticky-sweet bugginess.

I didn't make it more than five steps before Donovan came out. A solid, broad-shouldered, six-foot-two mass of frequently impenetrable emotions. Not impenetrable enough this time, though.

Even at a distance of half a parking lot, I detected two powerful sensations that crashed, one after the other, into my awareness.

One, he was hugely curious about why I was here.

And, two, he very much wished I hadn't been.

He walked up to me and cleared his throat. "Car trouble, Aurora?" He glanced at my hand-me-down, smoke-blue, five-year-old Buick Century, which had done nothing but purr contentedly during my drives around town. Donovan was the type to have noticed this, so I could tell he knew it wasn't the car.

I shook my head. "I need to show you something," I told him. "Privately."

A small flash of amusement quirked one corner of his mouth upward. I was surprised he allowed me to read this, especially since he knew I could. Surprised he was letting me see that one of his possible explanations for my presence was flirtatious in origin—even as he immediately dismissed the idea.

I rolled my eyes. "It's not like that," I murmured.

He pressed his lips together, but the amusement still simmered just beneath the surface. "Too bad. 'We're both *young* and *inconspicuous*,'" he said, parroting the hideously embarrassing words I'd said to him one night when I was a sophomore and had snuck into our brothers' secret high-school graduation party with my best friend Betsy. The guys had held it forty minutes away in St. Cloud so none of our parents would know.

I fought a blush. "We're not *that* young," I told him, trying to stand straighter and look older. "And we're not inconspicuous *here*."

"Ain't that the truth." He turned and motioned for me to follow him inside, clicking the shop's cool new garage-door opener so the second of the three garage doors came down behind us, rattling until it touched the concrete.

He led me into the back office and ushered me in. "You

want me to close this door, too? Snap the blinds shut?" He was mocking me, but there was a layer of concern beneath it. He knew something serious was up. In a town of 2,485 people, where you'd run into the majority of the residents a handful of times each week, I'd spoken with Donovan McCafferty in private exactly six times in the past five years.

Here's to lucky number seven.

"Yes to the door," I said. "No to the blinds."

He did as I asked and then leaned against the smudged once-white wall, crossed his arms and studied me. "What's this all about, Aurora?"

I nodded and pulled Gideon's journal out of my bag.

"I found this," I told him, explaining the odd circumstances of my discovery, and watched as his dark eyes narrowed. The curiosity of a few minutes before became heavily spiked with suspicion. He flipped through several pages of the journal, silent. He was processing all of this, I knew, but he didn't quite seem to get it. To be able—or willing—to take the appropriate intuitive leap. To allow himself to follow the fated path of the pinball.

So, I pointed again to the recently dated page and to Gideon's words on it, scrutinizing Donovan's face as he read it a second time. I saw every nuance of his reaction. Couldn't miss the two major transitions, shifting his expressions in slow motion like tectonic plates made visible. Incredulity hardening into doubt. Hope melding into anger.

"What makes you think this new date written down is even real?" he growled at me. "Your brother could've just scribbled it in the corner two years ago as a note for himself. Or somebody else could have written it. There are a hundred possible explanations. Finding this journal all of a sudden doesn't prove anything."

"I think it does," I said quickly, but very cautiously.

Insight into a guy's emotions was no guarantee I'd correctly predict his behavior. In Donovan's case, he was a human knot of tension and anger. I had no earthly idea what he'd do next, so I did my best to come across as super calm.

"I know this is probably difficult to accept," I said, "but I'm almost positive Gideon wrote in this recently and that he brought it back to Chameleon Lake himself."

Still, Donovan didn't believe me.

"Your brother is *dead*, Aurora. And so is Jeremy. You know that. We *all* know that. Otherwise, they would've come back by now." For a second, his voice broke, giving away the anguish behind the words. He tried to cover it up. "You show this thing to anyone and they'll think you're crazy. 'Oh, look, my brother wrote me notes from the grave,'" he said with full-on sarcasm. "'And, hey, sometimes he visits me at my house, too.' Yeah. Have fun convincing anybody of that."

"I'm not showing it to anyone else, at least not until I have an idea of what it all means," I snapped. "But try to imagine I'm right. Just *try*. You knew your brother best. Is there anything here that jumps out at you a little? Makes sense to you? Especially those technical terms. Can you figure out what they were working on?"

Donovan wasn't a person who took orders willingly, at least not from someone he didn't consider his direct superior, so, of course, he didn't answer any of my questions.

"Tell me *exactly* what you're planning to do with this." He held up the journal.

I shrugged. "I'm just trying to understand it." This was mostly truthful.

Donovan stared at me—his face moving closer to mine as he searched for whatever clue he was looking for in my expression. It was precisely *this* uncomfortable sensation of being so carefully observed that made me keep my distance from the guy. I was used to analyzing the minute movements, body language and facial changes of others. It was not, however, my idea of a good time to be the subject of such scrutiny myself. Thankfully, that rarely happened.

I knew Donovan didn't make a habit of reading reactions like I did, but he seemed to enjoy turning the tables on me whenever possible. He was one of the only people I'd ever met who instinctively knew from Day One that I possessed this heightened perceptiveness. A natural gift and, alternately, a curse. I'd been only twelve years old the first time we spoke, but he was guarded with me even then.

"Just read the page. Please." I motioned to the journal. "I looked up some of the words in an encyclopedia but, aside from figuring out that they're chemicals, they don't mean anything to me."

Ethylene glycol
Propylene glycol
Sulfuric acid
Sodium nitrate
Strontium nitrate
Atomized spherical aluminum
Bismuth subcarbonate
Ammonium nitrate
Sodium hypochlorite
Aluminum
Manganese dioxide
Sodium silicate
Zirconium powdery + 2 (+ 0)
Monday, April 19, 1976

J. & I drove to Crescent Cove
Potassium perchlorate
Sulfur
Antimony sulfide
M + 1 (+ 0), D + 10 (+ 0)

He read each of these hard-to-pronounce compounds aloud, along with the numbers and the mention of Jeremy and Gideon going to Crescent Cove. He shook his head. "This doesn't make sense. I don't know why they'd need most of it at all. A few of these are used for car engines, like the propylene glycol, so they might have needed that, but the others are common oxidizers."

I squinted at him. "In English, please?"

"Chemicals that blow things up. Potassium perchlorate and sodium nitrate are used as fuels for things like fireworks," he explained. "They're not hard to find. If our brothers wanted to get their hands on them, they wouldn't have had to drive three hours to Wisconsin. They could find them in St. Cloud. So, if they went to Crescent Cove two summers ago, it must have been for a different reason. To meet somebody, maybe."

Yes! And that was why I'd come here, risking sheer mortification and that pit-of-my-stomach unease, just to ask Donovan that question. I figured he'd know about stuff like this. And I could work with his conclusion. I could *do* something now... I only wished we'd had this clue two years ago.

But in my excitement, I made a stupid tactical mistake. "I can't wait to talk to that person," I murmured, realizing my error the instant the words were in midair. I tried to cover it up by smiling and shuffling my feet. Unfortunately, Donovan wasn't fooled.

His dark eyebrows rose slowly. "You're *going* there? When?"

I took a step back, regretting having requested the closed office door. We did not, perhaps, need *this* much privacy after all.

"Um," I said, shrugging and reaching for the journal. "It's not really set…"

Okay, this was a blatant lie. I had my excursion all planned, right down to my alibi for the weekend. No one would mind or even really notice. Not unless, like my brother, I happened to go missing the summer after *my* high-school graduation, too.

This worrisome thought distracted me. It was only for a second, but that was long enough for Donovan to snatch the journal from my grasp and say again, "Aurora, *when* are you going?"

Much as I preferred to keep him and everyone else out of it, maybe it would be wise to tell at least one person my real whereabouts. Just in case.

I sighed. "Tomorrow at noon. After I'm done with my shift at work."

"At the Grocery Mart?"

I nodded, not surprised he remembered that was where I had my part-time job. I'd felt his eyes track me when we were out in public. I knew he'd been aware of me all this time, just as I'd been aware of him. Unfortunately, the foolish crush I had on him only went one way. "I won't be gone long. Two days, at most."

In my mind, I'd already begun formulating the questions I wanted to ask in Crescent Cove. Seemingly innocent things that might draw out the responses I needed. I was sure if I asked just the right question to just the right person, the truth would be spontaneously revealed to me—by their hands, their eyes, their vocal tone, their posture. I didn't need their words. Soon, I'd know what happened to my brother and his best friend, and then this deadening sense of helplessness would have to stop.

Donovan was shaking his head again. With his army buzz-cut long gone, his dark hair grazed the back of his black crewneck t-shirt—a faded tribute to The Who.

Appropriate band for him. *Who are you...Donovan McCafferty? Who? Who?*

He flipped through a few more journal pages and glanced at the wall calendar, stroking one of his sideburns in thought. *"June's Muscle Car Babe!"* the calendar proclaimed, showing a tanned blonde, her hair feathered à la Farrah Fawcett-Majors, clad in a skimpy cherry-red bikini and leaning like a slutty go-go dancer across the hood of an equally cherry-red Ford Mustang. I gagged a little.

"Do you know Johansen's Diner in Alexandria?" he said suddenly.

"Sure," I replied. Everyone knew it. The owners served some of the better Norwegian specialties in the area.

"Good. There aren't many spaces out in front, but they have that free public parking garage across the street. Park on the second level. I'll meet you there at one p.m. tomorrow, and we'll drive to Crescent Cove together."

"What? No," I said, my irritation rising. "I'm not going there with *you*. I'm not going with *anyone*."

He stared at me for a very long moment. Opened the office door and motioned me out. He followed, locked up behind us and led me to the parking lot while clicking closed the third and last garage door. Then he pulled out his car keys and strode over to his Trans Am, turning to me a second before hopping in. "You sure as hell are, Aurora."

Too late, I realized he was still holding the journal. I broke into a run after him. "Donovan! Give me the—"

But he'd already started the engine and was partway to the street. He rolled his window down and added, "I need to read it tonight. You'll get it back tomorrow in Alexandria. Be there at one."

Then he sped away.

~*~

10:34 a.m.
CHAPTER TWO
Pasadena, California ~ Friday, August 15, 2014

No one else was home, of course, when I got the call that my twenty-eight-year-old son was missing.

"The Benson Plastics people are already here for the eleven o'clock presentation, but Charlie isn't," Gloria, the company's secretary, informed me, her piercing voice tinged with an edge of hysteria. I'd only spoken with the woman on the phone twice before, but I got the distinct impression that her circuits were forever at risk of being overloaded.

"He's not answering his cell?" I asked, surprised more than anything, actually, because both of my boys had their iPhones all but super-glued to their palms.

"Aurora, I've tried to reach him for an hour and a half," Gloria insisted, the shrillness in her tone rising like high notes in a chorus and dancing for dear life on the other end of the line. "There's no answer at home. His cell goes straight to voicemail. And I even called his girlfriend because she's his first contact. She has no idea where Charlie is either. You're his second contact, so I hope you'll know where we can reach him."

For a long, uncomfortable moment I was distracted by something ridiculous. The fact that I was only my son's *second* contact. Well, he was practically living with Cassandra, so I supposed it made sense that she was his first. But still...

Then the deeper meaning of the secretary's comments seeped in. *No one knows where Charlie is.* I tried to be calm, reasonable, rational and not like some TV sitcom mother who'd overreact to everything. But, naturally, given my family's history, that was impossible.

I fought back the panic and asked, "Was he at work yesterday?"

"Yes," Gloria said. "He was here when I left at four-twenty, and one of the department heads said he saw Charlie still working at his desk when *he* left at five. Martin, the team leader, was going to give the presentation to the plastics people this morning, but his wife called in saying he was sick with bronchitis. So, Charlie is the one who should be leading the meeting, but he didn't come in or call in an absence, and none of the managers here were told about any changes in his plans."

I understood instinctively that Gloria's first priority and much of her loyalty was to the company—Cornman, Grabher & Pressly—a financial firm my youngest son had worked at for these past three years. But it irked me that her focus remained on not disappointing "the plastics people," rather than on my son's safety.

"He never said anything to me about being gone from work today," I admitted, my mind reeling with that ever-present parental worry, which spun a dangerous path from my head to my gut. It settled there and began its slow, painful twisting.

Where is he? Is he okay? Why didn't he tell anyone where he was going? Unless, of course, he wasn't able to tell because he was hurt or in danger...or worse.

The questions started, and it was like 1976 all over again.

"I'll call his father and his brother," I told the secretary. "If either of them know anything, I'll contact you immediately."

"Thanks," the secretary said, but I could tell her attention was still fixed entirely on the wrong things, at least in my opinion. Then, finally, she added, "This just doesn't seem like him."

"No," I said. "No, it doesn't."

I hung up. I knew my son. He was a risk taker, an adventurous type, the kind of guy who loved thrill rides and fast cars and extreme sports. Different from his computer-obsessed older brother, who played Xbox when he was in the mood for *serious* activity and read ebooks when he was tired of programming things on his PC.

But Charlie wasn't irresponsible. If he was going to be gone from work, he would have told somebody. Maybe not me, but *someone*.

I thought back to when I'd spoken with him last—on Wednesday night. I'd asked him about his girlfriend Cassandra. *She's okay*, he'd said. And about work. *Yeah, it's fine*. And if he had any special plans coming up. *Nope*.

The ticking clock on the wall marked the passing minutes as my worry flooded the rest of my body. Ripples of dread meted out in sixty-second increments. Everything had seemed all right with him just two days ago but, then, kids often lied to their parents or, at the very least, withheld crucial information.

I should know.

Copyright 2014 by Marilyn B. Weigel. Twelfth Night Publishing. All rights reserved.

~*~

You can read more about **The Road and Beyond** on Marilyn's website (www.MarilynBrant.com) and follow along on Aurora & Donovan's journey with photos that Marilyn took from her own Route 66 Road Trip!

OTHER BOOKS BESTSELLING AUTHOR MARILYN BRANT

Contemporary Romantic Women's Fiction:
According to Jane
Friday Mornings at Nine
A Summer in Europe

Sexy Contemporary Romance:
On Any Given Sundae
Double Dipping
Holiday Man
The Sweet Temptations Collection (3-book set)
All About Us (a novella in the All I Ever Wanted anthology)
And look for the MIRABELLE HARBOR series—coming soon!
Book One: Take a Chance on Me
Book Two: The One That I Want
Book Three: You Give Love a Bad Name
Book Four: Stranger on the Shore
...and more...

Sweet Romantic Comedy:
Pride, Prejudice and the Perfect Match
Pride, Prejudice and the Perfect Bet
The Perfect Pair (2-book set)

Romantic Mystery:
The Road to You
The Road and Beyond (an expanded book-club version of The Road to You)

ABOUT THE AUTHOR

Marilyn Brant has been told she writes with honesty, liveliness, and wit (descriptors she's grown terribly fond of) about complex, intelligent women—like her friends—and their significant personal relationships. Although her favorite pursuits undoubtedly involve books, she proves she's not just a literary snob by confessing her lifelong fascination (read: obsession) with popular music, especially from the '70s and '80s, most flavors of ice cream, and a variety of sensuous body lotions/oils.

As a former teacher, library staff member, freelance magazine writer, and national book reviewer, Marilyn has spent much of her life lost in literature. She is the *New York Times* and *USA Today* bestselling and award-winning author of nine novels to date, and a lifetime member of the Jane Austen Society of North America. The Illinois Association of Teachers of English (IATE) selected her as their 2013 Author of the Year.

Her debut coming-of-age novel, *ACCORDING TO JANE* (Kensington, 2009), featuring the ghost of Jane Austen giving a young woman dating advice, won the Romance Writers of America's prestigious Golden Heart® Award and the Booksellers' Best, and it was named one of the "Top 100 Romance Novels of All Time" by Buzzle.com. Her second novel, *FRIDAY MORNINGS AT NINE* (Kensington, 2010), was a Doubleday and Book-of-the-Month Club pick in women's fiction. *A SUMMER IN EUROPE* (Kensington, 2011) was featured in the Literary Guild and BOMC2, and it became a Top 20 Bestseller in Fiction and Literature for the Rhapsody Book Club. The

Polish translation of the novel was released in June 2013.

She's also a #1 Kindle and #1 Nook bestseller, who writes fun and flirty romantic comedies, like her stories in *THE SWEET TEMPTATIONS COLLECTION*, that involve sweet treats, unexpected love, and large doses of humor. *THE ROAD TO YOU*—a coming-of-age romantic mystery—was selected as one of the Top 20 Best Books of the Year (December 2013) by The Reading Frenzy. Several of her novels will soon be available in audio CD/download from Post Hypnotic Press. Look for them and for more romantic fiction in 2015 and beyond!

Marilyn currently lives in the Chicago suburbs with her family. When she isn't reading her friends' books or watching old movies, she's working on her next novel, eating chocolate indiscriminately, and hiding from the laundry. Please visit her website: www.MarilynBrant.com.

www.ingramcontent.com/pod-product-compliance
Lightning Source LLC
Chambersburg PA
CBHW031447040426
42444CB00007B/1014